Governments and Markets in East Asia

The Asian economic crisis of 1997–8 had a dramatic impact not only on the region's economies but also on its politics. This book examines the relation between economic performance, elite cooperation, and political regime stability in the context of the Asian crisis. It argues that economic crisis is not the cause of greater political harmony or discord; rather, it serves as a catalyst that may encourage elites to cooperate or conflict depending on the particular circumstances at the time of crisis. It maintains that the political consequences of the Asian crisis varied according to the type of elite that existed in a crisis-stricken society. It goes on to consider the origins and socioeconomic impacts of the crisis in Indonesia, Thailand, Malaysia, South Korea, and the Philippines. It investigates the precrisis political contexts and elite configurations of these five countries, and considers what lessons can be drawn from their experiences. Overall, this book constitutes an impressive body of descriptive and theoretical material on the Asian crisis and the implications of economic crisis for elite behavior and political stability.

Jungug Choi is Assistant Professor at the Department of Political Science, Konkuk University, Korea. His main research interests include political party systems, electoral behavior and political economy in East and Southeast Asia.

Routledge Malaysian Studies Series

Published in association with the Malaysian Social Science Association (MSSA)

Series Editors:

Mohammed Hazim Shah, University of Malaya
Shamsul A.B., University Kebangsaan Malaysia
Terence Gomez, University of Malaya

The *Routledge Malaysian Studies Series* publishes high quality scholarship that provides important new contributions to knowledge on Malaysia. It also signals research that spans comparative studies, involving the Malaysian experience with that of other nations.

This series, initiated by the Malaysian Social Science Association (MSSA) to promote study of contemporary and historical issues in Malaysia, and designed to respond to the growing need to publish important research, also serves as a forum for debate on key issues in Malaysian society. As an academic series, it will be used to generate new theoretical debates in the social sciences and on processes of change in this society.

The *Routledge Malaysian Studies Series* will cover a broad range of subjects including history, politics, economics, sociology, international relations, geography, business, education, religion, literature, culture and ethnicity. The series will encourage work adopting an interdisciplinary approach.

Governments and Markets in East Asia

The politics of economic crises

Jungug Choi

Routledge
Taylor & Francis Group

LONDON AND NEW YORK

First published 2006
by Routledge
2 Park Square, Milton Park, Abingdon, Oxon OX14 4RN

Simultaneously published in the USA and Canada
by Routledge
270 Madison Ave, New York, NY 10016

Routledge is an imprint of the Taylor & Francis Group, an informa business

© 2006 Jungug Choi

Typeset in Times New Roman by Keyword Group Ltd.
Printed and bound in Great Britain by Biddles Ltd, King's Lynn

British Library Cataloguing in Publication Data
A catalogue record for this book is available from the British Library

Library of Congress Cataloging in Publication Data
A catalogue record for this book has been requested

ISBN10: 0-415-39902-5 (hbk)
ISBN10: 0-203-96864-6 (ebk)

ISBN13: 978-0-415-39902-9 (hbk)
ISBN13: 978-0-203-96864-2 (ebk)

To my mother and father in Seoul

Contents

List of tables

List of figures

Preface

This volume analyzes relations between economic performance, elite transformations, and regime stability in the five countries that were seriously affected by the 1997–8 Asian economic crisis: Indonesia, South Korea, Thailand, Malaysia, and the Philippines. I subject an array of descriptive material for each country to systematic analyses to determine whether the crisis intensified conflict or engendered cooperation among political elites. My point of departure is Stephan Haggard and Robert Kaufman's thesis that economic crisis increases political instability, while economic growth leads to political stability. I juxtapose this thesis with those of Barry Weingast, Karen Remmer, and others who argue that economic crisis may actually produce more stable regimes, as well as with Mancur Olson's claim that neither economic growth nor crisis is conducive to political stability.

My own position is that economic crisis by itself may encourage political elites in some contexts to cooperate but drive elites in other contexts toward greater conflict. I argue, in short, that economic crisis is not the *cause* of greater political cooperation or conflict. Rather, economic crisis serves as a *catalyst* for more cooperation or conflict under circumstances that I specify. To demonstrate this, I employ John Higley and Michael Burton's typology of political elites, and I classify elites in the five crisis-affected countries in three broad types: divided (Indonesia), fragmented (Philippines and Thailand), semi-consensual (Malaysia and South Korea). My contention is that the political consequences of the 1997–8 crisis varied according to which type of elite existed at its onset. This is similar to Juan Linz and Alfred Stepan's path dependence thesis in which various types of pre-transition regimes shape divergent prospects for democratic transition and consolidation.

Chapter 1 of my volume sets forth this theoretical framework, while Chapter 2 discusses the origins and socioeconomic impacts of the Asian crisis. Chapter 3 explores the five countries' precrisis political contexts and elite configurations. Chapters 4–6 deal with the three main country patterns: the Indonesian, the Filipino and Thai, and the Malaysian and South Korean. Chapter 7 concludes with a brief summary of my findings.

Most other studies of the Asian economic crisis deal with its economic or political consequences in a single country. Even when they cover several countries, they are edited volumes that deal with various aspects of the crisis without a common theoretical framework. Consequently, the existing literature about the Asian economic crisis lacks a systematic, cross-national, and comparative analysis.

Also, the greater portion of the literature focuses on economic issues such as how the crisis originated, why particular countries like Taiwan and Singapore were largely unaffected, why some countries turned to the IMF for help while others, like Malaysia, generally did not, and how the crisis affected regional economic cooperation through ASEAN and APEC. Even when the existing literature deals with the more political aspects of the crisis, it discusses the process of economic (i.e., corporate, financial, and labor) reform, or it addresses the issues of why some countries adopted a neoliberal economic policy regime and how successful they were in implementing neoliberal economic policies. In other words, the existing literature is primarily oriented toward specific economic policies and policymaking process. Consequently, it pays little attention to the direct effects of the economic crisis on political elites.

Yet, it is *political* elites that ultimately take the responsibility for making and implementing economic policies. Even when it comes to *economic* crisis, *political* elites decide on how to handle it. Moreover, political elites cannot be viewed as a constant variable. They are seriously affected by economic crisis, and, consequently, many of them rise and fall with it. Crisis-induced circulations and realignments of political elites, in turn, affect the direction and success of economic reform. The scant attention in the literature on the Asian economic crisis to its direct effects on political actors is all the more surprising because many pundits view the crisis as having originated in political elites' corrupt links to the business sector.

This volume is based on my 2001 PhD dissertation. This means, among others, that a large part of this volume was practically completed over the years of 1998–2000. A number of significant modifications, however, have been made for this publication, even though key research frameworks and arguments have been left intact. Most significant, a game-theoretical section in Chapter 1 has been deleted off to make it more accessible to those whose primary interest lies in substantial issues in Asian politics and economy. Also several other sections, especially in Chapters 4 and 6, have been rewritten to clarify and strengthen my arguments. Nonetheless, all these revisions are limited in the sense that they are far short of incorporating a number of new important political and economic developments in the region such as the rise of Thaksin's populist government in Thailand. I believe that separate works are required to deal with these recent political realignments. Part of Chapter 6 was previously published in "Ethnic and Regional Politics after the Asian Economic Crisis: A Comparison of Malaysia and South Korea," *Democratization* 10 (Spring 2003): 121–34 and is reprinted here with permission.

This volume would not have been completed without numerous personal, intellectual, and financial supports from others. My wife and two daughters have always been an unparalleled source of happiness to me. I also owe a debt of gratitude to my former dissertation committee members: John Higley, Tse-min

Lin, Melvin Hinich, Brian Roberts, and Patricia Maclachlan. In particular, I should like to single out Higley and Lin for special thanks. Higley tirelessly worked, despite his already tight schedules, to read numerous earlier drafts of this volume and willingly shared his invaluable insights and perspectives with me, and Lin kindly lent me strong personal support and encouragement as well as significant methodological suggestions. I am also immensely grateful to all those who were very helpful one way or another during my research field trip to Singapore, Malaysia, Indonesia, Thailand, Korea, and the Philippines in 2000. Part of my research including the field trip was supported by the MacDonald Dissertation Fellowship and the International Education Fee Scholarship of the University of Texas at Austin. I additionally appreciate very generous support and fine hospitality offered by the fellows and staff of the Center for East and Southeast Asian Studies at Lund University in Sweden during my 2001–2 postdoctoral fellowship: Michael Schoenhals, Roger Greatrex, Mason Hoadley, Lise Skov, Michael Tivayanond, Marina Svensson, Annie Troedsson, and Nina Brand just to name a few. I finally wish to thank series editor Edmund T. Gomez for his special interest in my work, as well as Peter Sowden and Tom Bates at Routledge for their kind help with this publication.

1 Introduction: economic crises, political elites, and democratic stability

The economic crisis that rolled across East and Southeast Asia in the late 1990s provides a good opportunity to reexamine the relation between economics and politics. One of the most interesting issues is whether regime types (authoritarian regimes, semi-democracies, and democracies) matter in dealing with economic crises. Are centralized authoritarian regimes better at coping with economic crises than decentralized democracies, in which policymaking is more likely to be influenced by those who suffer or benefit from policy choices? Alternatively, are democracies more resilient in economic crises than authoritarian regimes?

With regard to the primacy of economic forces, a major question is whether economic crises undermine political stability by intensifying political conflict or, ironically, does weathering crises actually produce greater political stability? Reflecting the economic difficulties in the wake of the communist bloc's implosion and the subsequent transition to market economies in eastern Europe, as well as the persistent economic crises that followed democratic transitions in Latin America during the 1980s, much attention has been given to whether economic crises destabilize new democratic regimes or make major political actors more accommodative and restrained.[1]

This volume focuses primarily on the causal flow from economics to politics, even though the reverse causal flow, from politics to economics, must inevitably be considered. My focus on the primacy of economics can be justified by taking into account another primary concern of this volume, which is the more general issue of how actors come to cooperate. Thus, this volume is not confined to political economy's customary concern with the relation between economics and politics; it goes beyond this to explore a central issue in formal theory (or positive political economy), the origins of cooperation among self-interested actors.[2] My question is whether economic crises promote cooperation and, if so, how? This question will be addressed together with the relation between economic crisis and political stability. The context is the Asian economic crisis of the late 1990s.

Crises, cooperation, and democratic stability

A significant portion of the literature on democratic transition and consolidation has concluded that cooperative attitudes and behaviors are essential for democratic stability, even though there are disagreements about whose cooperative attitudes and behaviors are most crucial. Scholars who use concepts such as social capital and civic culture focus on the general citizenry or masses.[3] By contrast, elite theorists make key decision makers who occupy strategically important positions in society the most crucial actors, and they think in terms of elite consensus instead of a broad civic culture or the wide distribution of social capital.[4] Nonetheless, all agree that some irreducible and significant degree of cooperative attitudes and behaviors is the basis of democratic stability.

Despite this agreement, there is not much research on what makes actors cooperate initially and then on a continuing basis. For example, after chapters of discussion about the contrasting traditions of civic engagement in the north and South of Italy, Robert Putnam leaves his question of why the two regions got started on such divergent paths unanswered:

> The hierarchical Norman regime in the South is perhaps readily explained as the consequences of conquest by an unusually effective force of foreign mercenaries. More problematical and potentially more interesting are the origins of the communal republics. How did the inhabitants of north-central Italy first come to seek collaborative solutions to their Hobbesian dilemmas? The response to that question must await further research, not least because historians report that the answer seems lost in the mists of the Dark Ages.[5]

Putnam is unable to specify the origins of the social capital and mutual trust that he presents as an alternative to the dreadful Hobbesian solution to dilemmas of collective action, that is, third-party enforcement. Putnam can only posit that if thick networks of mutual trust exist, they can be relied on to solve problems of collective action. In many places and times, of course, such networks do not exist.

One plausible source of initial cooperation is a serious crisis. In fact, it has been suggested that a way to break from tragic sub-optimal outcomes is via a crisis that upsets the existing equilibrium. For example, Barry Weingast observes that external events such as an economic crisis, an irresolvable civil war, or a new foreign threat are required for elite groups to move from an asymmetric equilibrium to a Pareto-optimal equilibrium.[6] One school in elite theory shares this view: a crisis triggers greatly increased elite cooperation via a sudden and deliberate elite settlement.[7] In addition, examining contemporary Latin American experiences, Karen Remmer observes that economic crises may not, after all, be destabilizing:

> Patterns of government formation in Latin America during the 1980s provide additional evidence of a trend toward consensus formation rather than political polarization. Far from evincing growing symptoms of political extremism and elite dissension, the 1980s were characterized by unprecedented efforts at achieving national political consensus.[8]

Not everyone agrees with this view of crises as primary origins of cooperation. One dissenting view is that economic crises deepen conflicts among political actors. Hard economic times make it difficult for political elites to satisfy their constituencies; good economic times, conversely, help reduce conflicts. Thus, Jeffry Frieden, looking at the same Latin American patterns as Remmer, notes that "while the pie was growing, there was little conflict over its distribution; once it began to shrink, political strife erupted."[9] Stephan Haggard and Robert R. Kaufman elaborate this view:

> Economic conditions will determine how stable and robust [a political] bargain is. Good times generate support. Economic crisis, by contrast, creates incentives for the private sector to defect from that bargain, increases the likelihood of political protest 'from below,' and reduces the capacity of ruling elites to manage the resulting distributive conflicts.[10]
>
> [Economic] growth eases the trade-offs associated with the organization of political support, in part by permitting compensation to negatively affected groups. More generally, growth can reduce the frustrations and conflicts resulting from inequality or other social cleavages, and can thus mute the tendency to political alienation and destabilizing social violence.[11]

Nonetheless, not everyone who believes that economic crisis intensifies political conflict also agrees that economic growth is conducive to deepening political conflict. There is, in fact, a minority view that economic growth, in particular rapid economic growth, also fosters political conflict. This is true especially when economic growth is accompanied by economic inequality. Mancur Olson is the most visible proponent of this view. He asserts that "rapid economic growth is a major force leading toward revolution and instability."[12] At the same time, Olson contends that rapid economic decline also contributes to political conflict. In his view, "it is economic stability -the absence of rapid economic growth or rapid economic decline- that should be regarded as conducive to social and political tranquility."[13]

Against the widespread view that economic growth contributes to political cooperation while economic crisis leads to political conflict, Carlos H. Acuna and William C. Smith present yet another model. Its most striking feature is the insertion of time into the economic–political relation: the effect of economic performance on political conflict varies over time. When economic conditions initially plummet, political tensions increase; however, this linear relation is reversed as economic crisis deepens. Conversely, during an initial stage of economic growth, political instability decreases; yet, when economic conditions further improve, political tensions increase.[14] If we focus on the latter stages of both economic crisis and growth, the Acuna–Smith model is exactly opposite to the position taken by Haggard and Kaufman as well as many other scholars.

Recent theories about democratic transition and consolidation also challenge the earlier literature that attributed democratic or authoritarian breakdown to economic crisis.[15] In particular, Juan Linz and Alfred Stepan hold that democracy, unlike authoritarianism, enjoys sufficient political legitimacy to withstand economic difficulties.[16] The survival of most new democracies in the midst of severe

Table 1.1 The effects of economic performance on political stability

	Increased political stability (consensus)	Increased political instability (conflict)
Economic growth	Haggard/Kaufman Frieden	Olson Linz/Stepan (authoritarian regime only)
Economic crisis	Acuna/Smith (initial stage) Acuna/Smith (latter stage) Remmer Weingast Higley/Gunther	Acuna/Smith (latter stage) Olson Haggard/Kaufman Acuna/Smith (initial stage) Linz/Stepan (if authoritarian regime, but not if democratic regime) Geddes (if military regime)

economic crises in Eastern Europe and Latin America during the 1990s, in contrast to the democratic breakdowns that occurred in Latin America during the 1960s, seems consistent with this thesis. Reviewing the large literature of democratic transition accumulated during the last 20 years, Barbara Geddes contends that the effect of economic crises on the survival of authoritarian regimes varies depending on authoritarian regime types (military, personalist, and single-party regimes).[17] From my perspective, however, it is more interesting that this new literature does not go further to argue that crises may actually consolidate democracy by unifying key political actors. This is the possibility that I want to explore.

Before discussing this, however, it will be useful to summarize the contending views of how economic crisis and growth affect political stability (or consensus formation). Table 1.1 arrays some of the most prominent views.

Instead of choosing one of these conflicting views of the relation between economic performance and political conflict, I adopt the neutral position that crises by themselves may either encourage political actors to cooperate or drive them into deeper conflict. This is, in fact, the conclusion that Ekkart Zimmermann and Thomas Saalfeld reach in their study of how the economic crisis of the 1930s affected six European countries:

> The economic crisis increased electoral volatility in all six countries, but led to electoral polarization and elite polarization only in Germany and Austria. Both countries failed to form a democratic national political consensus and, as a consequence, experienced a collapse of their democracies [while liberal democracies in Britain, France, Holland, and Belgium were maintained].[18]

My thesis is that crises are not the *cause* of political cooperation or conflict. Rather, they serve as *catalysts* for cooperation in certain conditions. It is the *conditions* in which crises serve as catalysts for cooperation that I want to

Table 1.2 Types of political elites

	(Elite integration)	
	Strong	Weak
Elite differentiation – Wide	Consensual elite	Fragmented elite
Elite differentiation – Narrow	Indeocratic elite	Divided elite

explore. Specifically, I intend to examine the underlying conditions and processes in which economic crisis leads to *political elite* consensus and, thus, to democratic stability. For this purpose, I identify two possible paths to political elite consensus – elite settlements and elite convergences – each of which involves a cluster of distinctive conditions. After examining these paths to elite consensus, I will explore another issue of how economic crisis affects political elites that are already fairly consensual.

Elite paths to democratic stability

Focusing on economic crises and concomitant changes in political elites require distinguishing types of political elites. There is, however, no agreed typology of elites in political science, and each typology that has been advanced has met with numerous objections. The most recent and perhaps the most serviceable typology is that of John Higley and Michael Burton, and it is this that I intend to employ. Higley and Burton distinguish four political elite configurations according to the extent of elite integration and elite differentiation: consensual, ideocratic, fragmented, and divided (Table 1.2). They observe as follows:

> Integration is extensive when there are inclusive formal and informal networks that tie elites together and give them direct and indirect access to the most important decisionmakers. Integration is also extensive when there is a political *modus operandi* and set of game rules about which elites agree and to which they adhere in their competitions and collaborations. Differentiation is extensive when elites are diversified organizationally, specialized functionally, and have significant autonomy from each other and from the state – in a word, when elites are substantially plural.[19]

Even though both ideocratic and consensual elite configurations involve strong integration and they embody different types of elite cooperation, I deal only with the consensual elite configuration because there is no instance of the ideocratic pattern among the five crisis-hit Asian countries that I study.

I also borrow from Higley and Burton their conceptions of two kinds of elite transformations: settlements and convergences. In both processes, divided or fragmented elites may suddenly, in settlements, or gradually, in convergences,

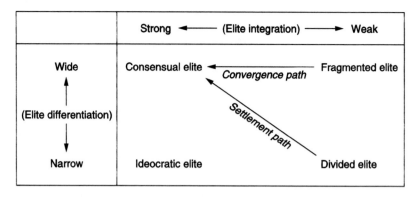

Figure 1.1 Elite configurations and two paths of elite change.

undergo transformations to the consensual type. But while I focus on these two paths to the consensual elite type, they are not the only paths to elite cooperation. Both in logic and in reality, there are at least two more paths: one from the fragmented elite configuration to the ideocratic and the other from the divided to the ideocratic. Yet, because I exclude the ideocratic elite configuration on the ground that there are no cases of it among the Asian countries I study, only the settlement and convergence paths to elite cooperation are relevant to my study (Figure 1.1).

Each path to a consensual elite involves different conditions. The distinction between these conditions corresponds to the distinction between divided and fragmented elites, that is, whether the existing elite is widely or narrowly differentiated. In other words, it is necessary to have separate models of elite consensus formation according to where a path starts. This is similar to Linz and Stepan's thesis about path dependence in which different pre-transitional regimes are displayed as providing different initial settings for post-transitional politics, and each carries different implications for democratic consolidation.[20] In the Higley–Burton scheme, to become a consensual elite a divided elite has to achieve not only strong integration but also wide structural differentiation. However, a fragmented elite has only to achieve strong integration, since it already displays wide differentiation. I will next discuss sequentially the conditions for the elite settlement path and those for the elite convergence path.

Path one to elite consensus: an elite settlement and its preconditions

As shown in Figure 1.1, an elite settlement is a process in which divided elites may suddenly undergo transformations to the consensual type. The elite settlement thesis holds that for a settlement to occur, first there must be a history of prior conflict in which all major elite groups have suffered heavy losses. Second, there must be a power stand-off between these groups, so that there is little chance for one group to prevail. Third, a crisis erupts and threatens to impose further costly losses on all major groups. Fourth, in the face of these expected losses, the principal opposing elites choose to resolve their most basic disputes and opt to cooperate to contain the crisis and also to overcome the long-standing enmities that are seen as contributing to it. As a result, a consensual elite configuration begins to emerge.[21]

In game-theoretic terms, the elite settlement thesis implies, as regards payoffs, that there is a hypothetical point below which any further or additional crisis-induced losses will be unbearable for each conflicting elite group. This game is not one of payoff maximization. Instead, players try to avoid the worst possible payoff; but above this lower payoff limit, each is willing to incur some loss to advance its interests. More important, the balance of power between opposing elite groups in the game prevents any one group from transferring its loss to another group. Concurrently, the relatively even distribution of power means that it is impossible for one group to obtain a disproportionate benefit or loss. If one group loses in the continuing conflict, so do the others. If one group gains by resolving the conflict, so do the others.

The idea of an elite settlement is sometimes presented in different terms, such as "a four-player game," "a transplacement," or "an extrication."[22] For instance, according to Juan Linz and Alfred Stepan, four-player games involve negotiated transitions between authoritarian regime soft-liners and opposition soft-liners who are both able to use and contain regime and opposition hard-liners, respectively. Linz and Stepan specify the conditions for a true four-player game: the regime soft-liners have to have sufficient autonomy from the regime hard-liners, and at the same time, the opposition soft-liners must be sufficiently strong to play the game against the hard-liners in their own opposition ranks. In other words, both moderate elite groups who negotiate with each other must be powerful enough to control their respective hard-liner elites.[23]

Linz and Stepan's theory of four-player games or pacted transitions rightly focuses on the power relations between game players. Yet, their four-player game requires moderates to be more powerful than hard-liners, and it pays less attention to the power relation between the two opposing moderate groups or between the regime and opposition camps more generally. By contrast, I argue that a balance of power between major elites that have engaged in protracted and severe conflict is the condition for successful negotiations between them.

Barry Weingast portrays this kind of elite pact as a sovereign-constituency transgression game.[24] In such a game, which is designed to explain the creation of self-enforced limited government, there are only three players: the state or king, and two citizens or societal actors. The key aspect of the game is that the state will not transgress against the citizens if both citizens are willing to fight jointly for the limits on the state. The game's outcome is "self-enforced" limited government in the sense that it is in the interest of the state or king to accept boundaries to its power once it is aware of the other players' willingness to jointly oppose any other outcome. Yet, this self-enforced limited government is only one of the multiple equilibria in Weingast's game. Analytically, there must be a focal point to ensure that the Pareto-optimal equilibrium emerges instead of other possible equilibria; constitutions, a leader, or a riot may serve as such a focal point.[25]

However, a focal point does not impel actors to move out of an existing asymmetric or non-Pareto-optimal equilibrium in the first place. To find out how and why actors break out of a non-Pareto-optimal equilibrium in the first place, Weingast advises us to go back to external shocks or some other exogenous force.[26] For Weingast, the genesis of cooperation cannot be simply reduced to a sudden coordination among actors who are willing to terminate their conflict if they are given a reliable mechanism of enforcement.

Weingast does not pay due attention to the existing power relation between actors in a conflict situation. Yet this is crucial for understanding why they move out of an existing non-Pareto-optimal equilibrium. Even in his three examples of an elite pact – England's Glorious Revolution settlement in 1688–9, El Salvador's peace accords in 1994, and the Missouri Compromise of 1820 – a balance of power among the actors in each conflict was crucial for reaching an elite pact. The Glorious Revolution settlement was possible only because the Tories' previously superior power position, which had been buttressed by the king (James II), was undermined by the breakup of the collusion between James and the Tories. This created a power balance between the Tories and the Whigs. With regard to the El Salvador pact, Weingast notes that "after years of war, both the insurgents and the regime recognized that neither could win." Finally, with regard to the Missouri Compromise, "the problem of sectional dominance was no longer one-sided, but reciprocal. Reciprocal vulnerability drove both sides [northerners and southerners] to resolve the problem."[27]

Some scholars nevertheless hold that a power balance is more likely to result in a temporary or sub-optimal solution to a conflict. For example, Adam Przeworski claims that when the power relation between political forces is balanced, there is

> no equilibrium in pure strategies, and one possible outcome is civil war . . . .
> Yet prospects of a prolonged conflict, of a civil war lasting perhaps for generations, are forbidding. Hence, political forces may be led to adopt some institutional framework, any framework, just as a temporizing solution.[28]

Przeworski goes on to claim that a stable institutional arrangement is reached when the power relation between forces is unknown, as behind a "Rawlsian veil."[29] This seems unrealistic to me. I argue that a mutually acceptable, and hence more long-lasting, set of institutions will be established only when the power relation of forces is balanced, because an institutional agreement reached in this situation serves no particular political elite group disproportionally.

To summarize, a power balance and a crisis jointly favor elite cooperation. In more detail, an even distribution of power between players is critical to inducing them to reach a compromise in the face of a crisis. Crises by themselves do not lead to cooperation unless they are accompanied by an even distribution of power among the major actors. Where there is a highly unbalanced distribution of power at the onset of a crisis, one of the players is well positioned to impose all or some of its loss on the other(s). Even if all players happen to suffer the same absolute magnitude of loss, the previously better-positioned player in the uneven distribution of power more easily bears the loss than the previously poorly positioned player.

We may hypothesize that a crisis transforms divided elites to consensual elites if and only if there is no grossly uneven distribution of power between the major elite groups before the crisis. To apply this theory of elite settlements to a particular country that has experienced a crisis, we first have to ask whether there existed a deeply divided political elite in the country before the occurrence of the crisis. If the answer is yes, the next question is whether the balance of power was more or less even between the groups making up the divided elite. If no even balance of power could be observed, then the prediction must be that the divided elite was unlikely to negotiate a settlement and move toward consensus. Indeed, it might have become fragmented if the dominant group lost control as a consequence of the crisis. Alternatively, the elite as a whole might simply have remained divided during and after the crisis. The main test case will be Indonesia, which clearly had a divided elite before the onset of the economic crisis in late 1997 as I will discuss in Chapter 3.

Path two to elite consensus: elite convergence and its preconditions

Fragmented elites may be transformed into consensual elites by following a convergence path that begins in a crisis and unfolds after it (Figure 1.1). Whereas an elite settlement takes place in a short period under circumstances in which the political influence of the mass publics is limited, elite convergence is a longer process in which mass electorates exert significant influence on the competition between the groups making up a fragmented national elite.

The process of elite convergence occurs when a broad electoral (more precisely, preelection) coalition is formed and then wins elections repeatedly. To avoid permanent exclusion from executive office, previously semi-loyal or anti-system parties are thus tempted to moderate their ideological positions, acknowledge the legitimacy of *existing* democratic institutions, and try to gain electoral victory within the existing competitive electoral rules. The crucial element in this path to a consensual elite is that parts of a fragmented elite form an electoral coalition powerful enough to threaten the virtually permanent exclusion of semi-loyal or anti-system parties from government executive power simply by adhering to the workings of minimal electoral rules. In short, elite convergence is achieved through the formation of a stable winning electoral bloc, a consequent narrowing of ideological differences, and eventually, the electoral victory of the previously dissident elites.

France from the formation of the Gaullist winning coalition in 1960 until the moderation of the Socialists in the 1970s and their electoral victory in 1981 is the paradigm case of an elite convergence.[30] The French elite convergence began with the formation of the Gaullist center-right elite coalition against the left and its victory in the National Assembly elections of November 1962. Thereafter, previously fragmented French elites were increasingly arrayed in two broad camps: the dominant center-right coalition, and the parties on the left including the Communists and the Socialists. Over the next 20 years, the electoral dominance of the center-right coalition gradually forced the leftist elites to reexamine their strategies, policies, and ideologies. By the mid-1970s, the Communist Party had abandoned its antisystem stance and accepted the existing electoral game rules that had been laid out by their former political opponents. To challenge the dominant center-right coalition, the Communists sought a rapprochement with the refurbished and newly moderate Socialists. The result was the Socialist–Communist Common Program for Government. After the Communists' withdrawal from the Program in 1978, the Socialists became the largest leftist party and they finally won the presidency, together with an absolute majority in the National Assembly, in 1981. Since then, though hardly free of the normal pushing and shoving of politics, French elites have repeatedly exhibited much restraint and moderation in their contests and, for the first time in French history, political institutions have been stable.

One big question with regard to this convergence path is how to form a *stable* dominant electoral bloc in the first place or why roughly half the previously conflicting political elites become united and remain so, thereby eventually pressing other political elites to moderate their positions to compete for government executive power effectively. This question remains unanswered although it is speculated that the initial formation of a dominant electoral bloc is most probably a response to a crisis or an attempt to manage a crisis. For example, the Algerian crisis of 1958 in France provided the initial conditions for the Gaullist bloc's formation.

Obviously, not every crisis initiates a convergence among fragmented elites. But convergence is more likely when fragmented elite groups, including antisystem groups, are located along an ideological spectrum or other linear political cleavage line. This does not mean, however, that there must be only one political cleavage line for an elite convergence to occur. All societies have several cleavage lines that often crosscut each other. The questions are, rather, whether one political cleavage line predominates over others, and what that predominant cleavage line is. A single issue dimension with no fixed center, such as ethnicity, is much less conducive to creating a point of convergence than is a single issue dimension that has a nonarbitrary center, such as a class-based, income-based, or ideological cleavage.[31] In this sense, a society whose most salient political cleavage is class opposition or income distribution is more propitious for democratic stabilization through elite convergence than one whose most salient political cleavage is ethnicity or regionalism.

Many scholars point out inherent problems of democracy in a society ridden with ethnic conflicts unless democratization is supported by particular institutions that discourage majority rule.[32] A frequently cited reason for the possible incompatibility of democracy and ethnicity is psychological in nature.[33] I share this view about the possible incompatibility of democracy and ethnicity, but I present a different reason for their incompatibility. An ethnic identity is qualitative and indivisible. Qualitatively different ethnic groups cannot be arrayed on a single linear line. Moreover, an ethnic cleavage does not have a single nonarbitrary center like an ideological one. On such a cleavage, there is no inherent center or left or right. This means that an ethnic cleavage has no center of gravity towards which disintegrating political forces converge.

It has already been shown amply by spatial theorists that when voters having single-peaked preferences are distributed over a single linear issue dimension, a median voter can never lose in a majority rule contest. In other words, political actors have a strong incentive to converge to the median point to win an election. Spatial theorists also prove that when there is more than one linear issue dimension, it is much more difficult to reach an equilibrium than if there is only a single linear issue dimension.[34] Here I make a slightly modified argument that even if the issue dimension is single, it is nearly impossible to reach a stable equilibrium unless the issue dimension has a nonarbitrary center. In other words, for the median voter theorem to be applicable, the single dominant issue dimension needs to be linear in the first place. When there are qualitatively different ethnic groups in conflict, they cannot be arrayed along a nonarbitrary linear line.

I also do not put as much weight on the crosscutting of cleavages as on the existence of a single dominant cleavage and its nature. A part of the literature, in particular, that on American politics, has put forward a different claim, to wit, that democratic stability is built on multiple issue cleavages that crosscut, instead of reinforcing, each other.[35] By contrast, I contend that the number of *salient* issue dimensions and the nature of the predominant issue dimension are more important than crosscutting dimensions. The two best-known propositions about the relation between political cleavages and democratic stability focus on the psychological cross-pressures that stem from the crosscutting of multiple issue dimensions or the extent of homogeneity in an ascriptive cleavage. One proposition is that "if there is not sufficient crosscutting between politically relevant cleavages, then democratic political organization is not likely to be stable." The other is that "if a society is either too homogenous or too heterogeneous over racial, linguistic, and religious cleavages, then democratic political organization is not likely to be stable."[36] Unlike the first proposition about crosscutting cleavages, I argue that what matters is the existence of a *single dominant* issue dimension. This implies that the *reinforcing or overlapping* of cleavages sometimes helps to moderate extreme positions, because it practically reduces the number of cleavages and, consequently, creates a simpler issue agenda.[37] Unlike social pluralists, on the other hand, I emphasize a *linear* cleavage dimension. The moderation of previously nonconciliatory issue positions does not depend on the degree of ethnic homogeneity (or heterogeneity) but on whether nonascriptive cleavages are more salient than ascriptive cleavages.

With regard to the Asian economic crisis, my analytical framework leads me to examine cleavage structures in countries with fragmented elites to determine whether there was a predominant political cleavage line before the crisis, and, if so, whether it constituted a linear issue dimension with a nonarbitrary center. If such is found, I will predict that the country was more likely to spawn the stable winning electoral coalition, that is, the initial step in an elite convergence. Of course, to provide a complete analysis of elite convergences, I also have to examine the status of anti-system parties. The test cases will be the Philippines and Thailand. As mentioned in Chapter 3, both countries had fragmented elites at the onset of the economic crisis in late 1997.

Economic crisis and the deepening of elite consensus

So far, I have discussed two paths through which elites become consensual as a consequence of a crisis: an elite settlement through which a divided elite is transformed into a consensual elite, and an elite convergence through which a fragmented elite becomes a consensual elite. However, what about elites that are already consensual before a crisis? Does an existing consensual elite survive a crisis or does it break apart into the fragmented or divided configuration? Such possible crisis-induced breakups of consensual elites are wholly unstudied. Even though consensual elites are in a better position to cope with a new crisis than fragmented or divided elites, they are not invulnerable to an unprecedented shock.

As discussed in Chapter 3, there is no case of fully consensual elite among the countries studied here. There are only the semi-consensual elites in Malaysia and South Korea to assess. Hence, I will ask whether and how the partial consensus among Malaysian and Korean elites either increased or decreased as a consequence of the severe crisis that both countries experienced in 1997–8. Put differently, I will not explore the underlying conditions for deepening elite consensus; instead, I will assess the Malaysian and Korean elites' resiliency in the face of that crisis.

It is not easy to classify precrisis Korea or Malaysia in terms of its elite configuration. For instance, some scholars rather view the Korean elite as fragmented and the Malaysian elite as divided. Other experts rather classify both as simply consensual.[38] There is some truth in either of these views. Considering these expected disagreements, here, it is good to offer a brief comment about the Malaysian and Korean elite configurations. I leave a detailed description of those configurations until Chapter 3, where I deal with all five countries' political circumstances before the economic crisis, focusing specifically on their elite configurations.

Before the onset of the economic crisis in 1997, a supermajority elite group, based in the National Front (or, formerly, the Alliance), had continuously ruled Malaysia. The national elite as a whole lacked wide structural differentiation but it still exhibited relatively strong integration. Obviously, the precrisis Malaysian elite was not of the ideocratic type since there was without a single political ideology akin to state-socialism or fascism. Rather, Malaysian elite integration derived at least in part from the omnipresent threat of ethnic violence in an eminently multiethnic society. Moreover, the extent of elite differentiation was much wider than in state-socialist or fascist systems, while elite integration was not as centralized and rigid.

Neither was the precrisis Malaysian elite configuration divided. The dominant Malaysian elites had constantly legitimized themselves through regular and significantly free popular elections. Even though these elections had not been completely free, opposition parties had never boycotted them, and some opposition groups had occasionally been part of the ruling alliance. This implies that Malaysian elites were integrated to an extent greater than is characteristic of divided or fragmented national elites.

But the precrisis Malaysian elite was not entirely consensual either, primarily because the degree of elite differentiation was not impressively great. This is why, unlike in other pluralistic democracies, the National Front was the perennial winner, even if its margin of victory varied from election to election. The Malaysian elite, in other words, did not operate a democracy in which "organized uncertainty" is a central feature: electoral outcomes were instead certain, and rules of the game had arbitrary aspects. Moreover, the absence of organized uncertainty in Malaysia derived importantly from the National Front's strong and unwavering electoral support by the largest ethnic community, the Malays.

In sum, before the economic crisis of 1997–8 the Malaysian elite was semi-consensual: elite integration was quite strong, but elite differentiation was not very wide. To a lesser degree, this was also true of the South Korean elite. Of course, South Korea's political system was more competitive and pluralist than Malaysia's, and its new democracy successfully and gradually got rid of one of the common threats to democracy, that of a military coup, before the economic crisis hit the country. Nevertheless, as discussed in Chapter 3, Korean elites did not have significant autonomy from each other and from the state, even though business elites' autonomy from the state steadily strengthened after the democratic transition in 1987. More important, the dominance of regional voting cleavages involved rigid linkages between the political elites and voters. This rigidity in individual voting further lessened elite differentiation, despite the free electoral contests at the system level after 1987. The persistence of regionally hegemonic political parties prevented the evolution of policy-oriented political parties that would be more widely differentiated. In addition to the rigidity of regional voting, the concentration of national assets in a few industrial oligarchs or chaebols kept elite differentiation quite limited.

Concerning the impacts of the Asian economic crisis on Malaysia and South Korea, I intend to assess the postcrisis political circumstances in both countries in terms of elite consensus to tell whether the crisis had the effect of consolidating the already fairly consensual elites. For Malaysia in particular, it will be important to ask whether the crisis resulted in a breakup of the Malaysian supermajority elite group and whether it decreased the magnitude of rigid ethnic voting among the Malaysian mass public. If this group broke up and the magnitude of ethnic voting decreased as a result of the crisis, elite consensus and cooperation would actually be enhanced. Likewise, to see whether the economic crisis deepened elite consensus in Korea, I will focus on how it affected elite differentiation and rigid regional voting cleavages. I will seek to determine if the rigid regional voting became more fluid in the wake of the economic crisis, whether the business sector became more autonomous from the state, and whether national assets became less concentrated in the hands of chaebols. Autonomous societal actors, detachments from regionally hegemonic parties, and decentralized national assets deepen elite consensus by enhancing elite differentiation in Korea.

Outline of the volume

The Asian economic crisis is described and analyzed in Chapter 2. There I focus on its underlying causes and socioeconomic consequences, as well as the national responses to it. In Chapter 3, the precrisis political conditions of the five countries that were hardest hit by the crisis are reviewed: Indonesia, South Korea, Thailand, Malaysia, and the Philippines. I will highlight the precrisis elite configurations in all five, and I will classify these as divided (Indonesia), fragmented (Philippines and Thailand), and semi-consensual (Malaysia and South Korea). Using this classification, in Chapter 4, I will analyze prospects for an elite settlement in Indonesia in the midst of crisis and why none occurred. In Chapter 5, I will analyze prospects for elite convergences between the two fragmented national elites, the Filipino and Thai. In Chapter 6, I will ask how economic crisis affected elite cooperation among the already semi-consensual Malaysian and Korean elites. This volume concludes in Chapter 7 with a brief summary of my findings and their implications.

2   The outbreak of the Asian economic crisis and its socioeconomic consequences

Features and causes of the economic crisis

To provide some preliminary knowledge of the Asian economic crisis, this chapter summarizes (1) why the crisis erupted, (2) how actors reacted to it, and (3) what its main socioeconomic consequences were. Even though the causes and socioeconomic outcomes of the crisis are not my major concern, the causes are, to some extent, relevant to the key issue of this volume, namely, elite cooperation. For the actors to cooperate, they need to perceive a crisis as a serious *common* threat. In general, this perception is more readily formed when the causes of a crisis are exogenous, such as a foreign military threat. At the end of this chapter, I also discuss why I view the Philippines as a crisis case and include it in this study, even though others might disagree.

The economic crisis in East and Southeast Asia in the late 1990s had some notable characteristics. First, no one expected it; hence, the crisis came as a great shock. Before the crisis, almost every macroeconomic indicator in the region was registering strong economic performance. This could be seen in high rates of GDP growth and national savings and low rates of unemployment. Figure 2.1 arrays the strong economic growth rates in the region, which slowed somewhat in the mid-1990s.[1] The economic crisis thus occurred in countries that had been highly touted as models of economic development for other developing countries, except the Philippines.[2]

Second, the crisis occurred not in a single country but in the whole region. By contrast, the Mexican economic crisis of 1994–5 was confined largely to Mexico. The Asian crisis started in Thailand and spread quickly to neighboring Malaysia, Indonesia, and the Philippines, as well as more distant South Korea.[3]

Third, the crisis occurred in a politically heterogeneous set of countries. The hardest-hit countries, such as Thailand, Indonesia, and South Korea, had quite different types of political regimes. Thailand had a regime that had long oscillated between democratic and military forms – a very unstable regime. Indonesia had an overtly authoritarian regime. Finally, South Korea had a democratic regime in place since 1987. So it is impossible to attribute the crisis to a particular form of political regime.

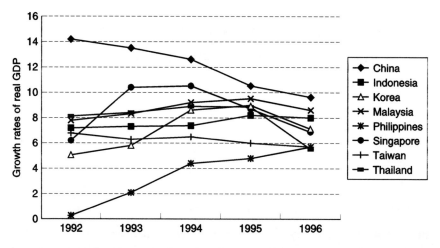

Figure 2.1 Asian economic growth before the regional crisis.

Source: The Statistics and Data Systems Division at the Economics and Development Resource Center of Asian Development Bank, http://internotes.asiandevbank.org. The figures are in constant prices.

However distasteful they may be, authoritarian regimes do not necessarily prompt economic crises. Some politicians, including South Korean President Kim Dae Jung, believe that authoritarianism was responsible for the Asian economic crisis.[4] Stephan Haggard points to some inherent weaknesses of authoritarianism such as the risk of arbitrary action, the lack of transparency in business-government interactions, and uncertainties in leadership successions. At the same time, he emphasizes the purported advantage of democracy in its self-correcting mechanism for voting out incompetents and bringing reformers into government.[5] Yet, in addition to the fact that a number of democracies had broken down amid economic crises earlier, a presidential democracy, as in South Korea and the Philippines, has fixed terms that do not lend themselves to voting out incompetents quickly. The holding of presidential elections within a year of the outbreak of crisis in South Korea and the Philippines were purely accidental. Moreover, Thailand's parliamentary democracy did not hold a new election to replace its incumbent coalition government; instead, there was a simple realignment of the governing coalition.

Fourth, the crisis was initiated by a steep devaluation of local currencies against the US dollar. Figure 2.2 portrays how much each local currency in Asia was devalued. Indonesia was hardest hit by the currency crisis among the eight countries in the figure: Indonesia, Korea, Thailand, Malaysia, the Philippines, Taiwan, Singapore, and Japan. The Korean, Thai, Malaysian, and the Philippine currencies were also seriously devalued. Among this middle-range group, the Philippines peso was the least affected, and the Korean won the most affected. As compared to these five currencies, the Taiwan, Singaporean, and Japanese

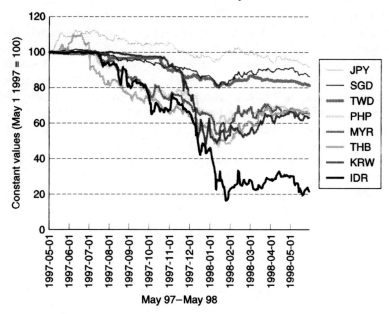

Figure 2.2 Foreign exchange rates of eight Asian currencies against the US dollar from May 1997 to May 1998.

Source: Pacific Exchange Rate Service, http://pacific.commerce.ubc.ca.

currencies were only moderately devalued. Other economic problems, such as soaring interest rates, inflation, and unemployment, only followed the currency devaluations. In this sense, the crisis was different from previous Latin American debt crises, even if it was closely related to unmanageable amounts of (mostly private sector) debt. In addition, the pattern of the Asian crisis, which began with the meltdown of local currencies, was different from eastern European cases, in which the sudden political collapse of state-socialist regimes largely preceded socioeconomic crisis.

There are widely varying views about why the Asian crisis occurred. Some tend to emphasize its external causes, viewing the crisis as attributable largely to the unpredictable movements of international capital.[6] On the other hand, some hold that the crisis testified to the failure of the Asian economic model and its fundamentals.[7] Still others think that the crisis was an instance of *market* failure, that is, a failure of international finance capital markets. They tend to blame excessive financial and market liberalization.[8] Or again, some believe that the crisis was simply another chapter in the global tendency of states to retreat from markets.[9] For these observers, strong state intervention in markets was the problem. The decline of state intervention had previously been seen in the total collapse of a planned economy in the former Soviet bloc; it had also been seen in the retreat from Keynesianism among the economically advanced Western countries.[10]

The dominant view holds that the crisis was primarily caused by domestic factors in debtor countries. For instance, inexperienced local financial institutions and their mismanagement of credits are often blamed. Although a significant proportion of the credits given by international banks were short-term, local banks loaned this borrowed money to their clients on long terms. Still worse, some of the borrowed money was spent on nonproductive sectors such as property assets and on political funding and kick-backs. Finally, even where borrowed money was spent in productive sectors, it was often invested in identical projects, which caused overproduction both in region and in particular countries.[11]

Against the dominant view that emphasizes the primary responsibility of domestic actors and institutions, I hold to the view that the crisis arose, primarily, from unprecedented massive attacks by external currency speculators on financially vulnerable countries. In other words, local financial institutions did not initiate the crisis; rather, they were more its victims.[12] A limited International Monetary Fund (IMF) study indeed confirms that hedge funds were responsible for the initial Thai currency devaluation.

> A study by the International Monetary Fund revealed that these funds took up large positions against the baht two months before the de facto devaluation of the currency on July 2, Barry Eichengreen, IMF's senior policy advisor, told a media briefing here [Washington]. "Sources of evidence point to the fact that some macro hedge funds had large positions against the baht in the summer of 1997," Eichengreen said. "It appears to us that hedge fund positions against the baht were built up gradually but they turned quite large only in the last two months prior to the Thai devaluation," he added. [13]

Yet, due to the secretive transactions of international speculative capital and the lack of much data about them, it is beyond this volume's ability to analyze what speculators did or did not do. Here, the discussion is instead focused on the international factors that contributed to the financial vulnerability of local economies. Many of these factors were well beyond the control of local economic actors and governments.

Economic vulnerabilities

The economic vulnerability of Asian countries, which increased the likelihood of being attacked by speculators, had several components. It was more than a simple matter of weak local financial institutions. The primary component was that the unprecedented economic growth in Asia had been heavily debt-financed. A tremendous absolute amount of debt was the dark side of Asia's brilliant economic performance during the 1980s and early 1990s. The poor economic performance of the US economy and the high savings and weak domestic demand of the Japanese economy in the late 1980s and the early 1990s had driven out their worst-performing holders of capital to Asia's developing economies. Figure 2.3 shows that after 1988 or 1989, the total amount of debt in South Korea, Thailand,

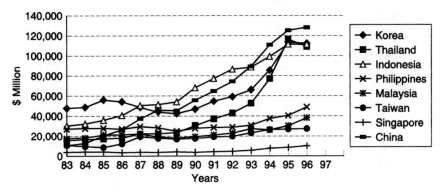

Figure 2.3 Total identified debt in Asian countries.

Sources: The 1985–1995 data come from OECD, *External Debt Statistics: Resource Flows, Debt Stocks, and Debt Service, 1985–1996* (Paris: OECD, 1997). The 1996 data are from OECD, *External Debt Statistics: The Debt of Developing Countries and CEECs/NIS at end-December 1996 and end-December 1995, 1997* ed. (Paris: OECD, 1997). The pre-1985 data come from OECD, *Financial and External Debt of Developing Countries: 1991 Survey* (Paris: OECD, 1992).

and Indonesia, which were the hardest-hit countries, had continuously and dramatically increased.

Although China had the largest amount of debt in Asia, it was not attacked by speculative capital. One reason was its tightly controlled foreign exchange market, and a second reason was its possession of the largest or second largest amount of foreign exchange reserves in the world.[14] Two moderate crisis cases, the Philippines and Malaysia, accumulated a relatively small amount of foreign debt. Malaysia was the country that had relied most heavily on foreign direct investment, rather than debt financing, before the crisis broke out.[15] Long before the crisis began, the Philippine economy was under IMF economic trusteeship.[16] Unlike other Asian countries, the Philippines' economic performance was not impressive until the few years immediately before the crisis, as seen in Figure 2.1. Hence, it was not treated as an example of the Asian economic model, which featured highly debt-financed and export-driven economic growth.

The vulnerability that arose from extreme exposure to international financial markets was reinforced by the fact that a significant proportion of total debt was short-term financed. The ratio of short-term to total debt was especially high in the three hardest-hit countries, South Korea, Indonesia, and Thailand. Figure 2.4 shows the proportion of short-term credit compared with total debt in December 1996. This does not mean, however, that the international financial institutions or markets that provided short-term credits caused the financial crisis. Rather, they contributed to its deepening by withdrawing their mature credits as a reaction to the initial devaluation of local currencies and the consequent disappearance of investor confidence in local debtor countries. Speculative attacks by "hot money" on local currencies triggered the crisis, even if the region wide effect was not intended or expected by the attackers.

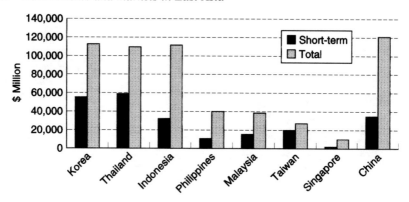

Figure 2.4 Short-term debt in Asian countries (December 1996).
Source: OECD, *External Debt Statistics*, 1997 edition.

It is important to observe that the high ratio of short-term debt was a rational response to international financial markets. Local actors preferred short-term financing because interest rates for short-term credits were usually lower than for long-term credits. In addition, no one expected the sudden collapse of booming Asian economies. Only with hindsight can one say that it was irrational for financial actors in the Asian countries to have chosen such risky financing.

A third international component that put much pressure on local currencies to devalue was the unilateral devaluation of China's currency in 1994.[17] After mid-1994, the Southeast Asian countries whose currencies were not devalued, lost much of their competitiveness in export markets and international capital markets. The Southeast Asian countries and China had similar export items based on cheap labor, such as textiles, and they occupied proximate positions in the international division of labor. As a *Washington Post* article reports,

> In the past two years, pushed by foreign investments and booming exports, China's foreign exchange reserves have nearly doubled. The $130 billion reserves of the People's Bank of China are evidence of, as H. Ross Perot puts it, the huge sucking noise moving industries from all over Southeast to Chinas.[18]

Declining competitiveness contributed to decreased economic growth rates in Southeast Asian countries.[19] For instance,

> Thailand's loss of competitiveness in labor-intensive products became very apparent in 1996, when total exports declined by 0.2 percent, compared with increases by over 20 percent per annum in previous years. Exports of some key items, such as medium to low end garments and shoes, declined by about 30–40 percent in 1996.

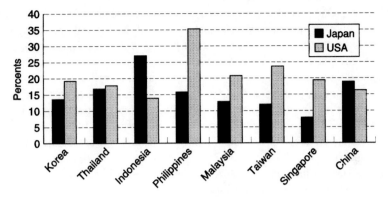

Figure 2.5 Exports from Asian countries to Japan and the USA before the crisis.

Source: Economist, *The Economist Pocket World in Figures 1998* (New York: John Wiley & Sons, 1997). Data refer to the year ending 31 December 1995.

To a lesser degree, this was also true of South Korea, which had a more advanced economic structure than the Southeast Asian countries.

A fourth pressure on the value of local currencies came from a power shift in the international economic structure, specifically, in the economic power relationship between Japan and the USA. By the mid-1990s, the sluggish economic growth of Japan and the recovering US economy, and the consequent reversal in their bilateral power relationship, made the Japanese yen weaker against the US dollar. One of the implications of the yen's weakening was that other Asian local currencies, whose values were fixed to the US dollar, became substantially overvalued. This took place when their economies were increasingly dependent on the Japanese economy, *vis-a-vis* the US economy, as an export market, as shown in Figure 2.5. To regain their economic competitiveness, the Southeast Asian and Korean currencies needed to be depreciated.

A final international factor that contributed to the capital exodus from Southeast and East Asia was the availability and attractiveness of other capital markets. In particular, the reviving US economy was a major alternative for capital that had earlier been invested in Asia. As a *Washington Post* report says,

> Much of the investment capital that has been fleeing from Asia has sought the safe haven of the U.S. bond market, driving interest rates below 6 percent. Already corporations and homeowners are rushing to refinance their debt, freeing up cash that could spur the economy through increased consumer spending and capital investment.[20]

Had this not been the case, foreign capital in Southeast and East Asia would more likely have been trapped there, and consequently, there would have been no other choice but to share the costs of financial adjustment in Asian countries. But this was not so. One observer complained about the consequent strong bargaining power of creditors as follows: "Debtors are not allowed to talk, but to agree."[21] The weak bargaining power on the part of the Asian debtor countries invalidates the previously convincing Latin American maxim that "If you owe your banker a thousand dollars, he owns you; if you owe your banker a million dollars you own him."[22] Accordingly, international banks and creditors did not absorb financial losses stemming from the crisis; instead, they simply continued their business unscathed.[23] They forced local debtors and the general public to bear all the costs. Moreover, local banks and financial institutions were blamed for their moral hazard.

In sum, against the dominant current view that domestic actors or financial and political institutions were responsible for the crisis, I emphasize the international factors that increased the crisis-hit countries' economic vulnerabilities to speculators' attacks and yet were beyond the control of domestic actors or institutions. The main causes of the crisis were to be located in the international economic structure. Even though I agree with the dominant view that the restructuring of domestic institutions was (and remains) necessary, this was less to prevent the recurrence of a crisis than to *reduce the negative impact* of a crisis once it breaks out.

Socioeconomic responses and effects

Since many books and articles about the socioeconomic effects of the crisis and the local socioeconomic responses to it have appeared, I will only point to the most notable features and trends during the first two years after the crisis broke out, although the longer-term trends might change.[24] One of the principal responses to the crisis was prevalent 'self-criticism,' even though the crisis was caused mainly by international capital movements. Consequently, most of the countries under attack did not blame the attackers to the extent that they might have done before. Put differently, there were few strongly nationalistic reactions to the crisis. The exception was Malaysia. Prime Minister Mahathir warned, for instance, that liberalization, deregulation, and globalization would "enrich the already rich at the expense of the poor."[25] But in spite of its prime minister's strong anti-imperialist rhetoric, Malaysia also remained loyal to IMF-style policies for more than a year after the crisis began.[26]

More generally, however, almost no one voiced strong dependency complaints; instead, each country tried to become more incorporated into a world market that was dominated by the United States.[27] Rather than protecting their domestic capital from external attack, most countries sought to open their economies further to foreign direct investment. This was in contrast to the nationalistic responses to the debt crisis during the late 1970s and early 1980s, in Latin America and to a lesser degree in Asia. In that earlier period, the idea of opening markets to foreign products, not to mention foreign investment, was a taboo. By the late 1990s, however, Asian governments not only did not hesitate to open their markets to foreign products but also competed for foreign capital in the form of both loans and foreign ownership, and this competition was intensified by the crisis.[28]

The crisis-hit countries also did not much dispute the fact that business and labor in debtor countries, as opposed to creditor banks and countries, had to bear virtually all of the costs. International creditors did not have to write off any of their credits, unlike in earlier downturns.[29]

The Asian countries displayed a more or less uniform policy response to the crisis. Their policies were coordinated, even dictated, by the IMF. The IMF's initial policies were mainly designed to strengthen market mechanisms and reduce government intervention in the local economies. In detail, these policies called for smaller governments and larger government budget surpluses by cutting government subsidies. The IMF also demanded lower growth rates, freer foreign exchange markets, more transparent transactions in local businesses, higher interest rates, and more flexible labor markets. Finally on the IMF's agenda was the restructuring of domestic financial institutions, to include closing some of them.[30]

The IMF's market-oriented measures to stem the Asian economic crisis were the opposite of those taken in the Great Depression, which marked the end of classical liberal capitalism. The Asian crisis and the measures to combat it produced several clear short-term effects, though their long-term effects are not as clear and remain in dispute. First, because the local currencies had been devalued, imported products and parts became quite expensive. This, in turn, caused relatively high rates of inflation and increased costs of production. In contrast, local items made with local parts and materials became much cheaper and more competitive in foreign markets. Owing to reduced domestic demand for foreign items, in combination with the increased export competitiveness of local products, the crisis-stricken countries experienced immediate trade surpluses. In Thailand, for instance, "The central bank announced its seventh consecutive monthly current account surplus of 1.48 billion dollars for March [1998]."[31]

Second, the combination of increased prices for imported parts and higher interest rates drove many local businesses into bankruptcy. The depreciated local currencies also contributed to high bankruptcy rates. This was especially true of those companies or organizations that were especially vulnerable as the result of large unhedged loans denominated in foreign currencies. Even some sound businesses went bankrupt under the severe financial crunch.

Third, as a result of the closing of many businesses and the unfavorable business environment, unemployment rates became high by modern Asian standards. This was in part due to the closing of some bad but also some good businesses and in part to massive layoffs of surplus labor by the businesses that kept going. The already bad unemployment rate became worse since there were not many new job openings for new entrants to the labor markets, in particular university graduates. At the same time, traditionally secure jobs in government offices and government-owned or controlled businesses were no longer protected. Governments tried to reduce their work forces and, at the same time, privatize their services and businesses. They also terminated or reduced subsidies for a variety of social organizations and activities, which, in turn, undermined their activities or reduced their budgets and personnel. These cuts in budgets and personnel across the public and private sectors resulted not only in worsening levels of unemployment and poverty but also in increasing economic inequality. In Indonesia, for instance, "As of March [1998], the government estimated 8.7 million people unemployed, nearly 10 percent of a total workforce of 90 million and double the total of June 1997." The World Bank estimated that 20 percent of Indonesia's 200 million people would be living in absolute poverty as a result of the crisis, compared with 11 percent in 1997."[32] A separate report confirms that postcrisis Korea experienced the increasing income gap between different income groups. In detail, the 1998 first quarterly income of the upper ten percent income group increased by 3.2 percent while the lower ten percent income group suffered 20.2 percent of loss in income during the same period, compared to the one-year earlier levels.[33]

Fourth, the depreciation of local currencies and the collapse of financial markets made national assets cheaper and more vulnerable to hostile and non hostile takeovers by risk-taking foreign capital. Thus, an important effect of the crisis was increased foreign ownership of domestic economic activities in both production and distribution. This increased foreign ownership was reinforced by Asian governments' and private businesses' aggressive attempts to attract foreign capital or sell local government projects and private businesses to foreigners. This buyer's market, overcrowded with sellers, further reduced the values of Asian domestic assets that had already been lowered by the currency devaluations. Each country tried to do the same thing – sell their national assets – but the number of willing buyers was limited.

Finally, even if the IMF economic guidelines or impositions sought to make governments smaller, government debts increased. The reason was that governments came to shoulder the costs of private economic actors' adjustments to the new economic environment. The governments were forced to pay creditors and depositors on behalf of bankrupt private businesses and financial institutions. At the same time, they also issued bonds to tackle soaring unemployment and other social problems in the wake of the crisis. For example, in 1998, the South Korean government planned to issue state or public bonds amounting to about 40 billion dollars or 52 trillion won in total.[34] The rapid increase in government debts was an important change because the Asian governments had not been in debt before the crisis; on the contrary, their financial positions had been strong.

In sum, despite the external factors that played the crucial role in causing the crisis, liberal policymakers in the crisis-hit countries did not blame international actors or institutions for the crisis but tended to perceive domestic institutions or actors as primarily responsible. They did not dare to ask the foreign creditors to write off their debt. They accepted the IMF-imposed liberalization policies without much hesitation. They sought to be more engaged in a US-dominated global economic system by further liberalizing their markets and standardizing local business conventions or institutions to fit the world system. Amidst this liberalization and strong self-criticism, local businesses and institutions that did not fit well into this new environment died out. Other local businesses were taken over by foreign capital. The IMF policies that emphasized more transparent and more liberal business practices and that did not pay as much attention to poverty alleviation contributed to widening economic inequality. The local governments not only took over the private debt that the foreign creditors refused to write off but they also shouldered the financial burdens required to liberalize the nonstandardized local institutions and buttress their falling economies by ameliorating increased poverty. As a result, the Asian governments rapidly became overloaded.

An excursus on the Philippines

Before concluding this chapter, some remarks are necessary about the case of the Philippines. It is obvious that the Philippines underwent a *currency* crisis, as was shown in Figure 2.2, even though the peso was slightly less devalued than the Malaysian ringgit. However, whether this currency crisis led to a *financial* crisis and to a still larger *economic* crisis in the Philippines is not self-evident. This is why some scholars compare the postcrisis Philippines to postcrisis Taiwan.[35] In other words, they think that the case of the Philippines was closer to Taiwan (which remained only on the periphery of the crisis) than to Malaysia or the other seriously affected countries. It is true that the Philippines was the least affected of the five countries displayed in Table 2.1. Yet, its currency and exchange markets were as hard hit as Malaysia's or Thailand's. The crisis also stifled the growth rate that had started to take off before the crisis. Although the absolute private consumption level did not turn negative,[36] the crisis pulled down the consumption level that had been reached right before the crisis. Other key economic indicators show that the crisis reversed the gradually improving economic conditions in the Philippines. In other words, the moment that the Philippines was about to cast off its sluggish economic image and become a kitten, if not a tiger, the crisis hit it. Consequently, I include the Philippines in this study.

Conclusion

Despite some dissenting minority views, most policymakers in the crisis-hit Asian countries did not view the crisis as primarily external in origin. The prevalent view was that illiberal or corrupt domestic institutions and actors were responsible for the crisis and had to be reformed to better fit the neoliberal global economy. Political leaders and their advisors took advantage of the crisis to expand their neoliberal agenda. The international creditors, including the IMF, strongly supported those neoliberal policies that were aimed at replacing the earlier state-led economic growth regimes with market-oriented and open economies. The successful implementation of such neoliberal policies presumably allows foreign capitalists to infiltrate more easily into the somewhat closed Asian economies. Yet, the Asian governments turned out to be more powerful *vis-a-vis* their domestic business actors, although not *vis-a-vis* foreign capitalists, because they took all the financial and other institutional reform initiatives and controlled the resources that were necessary to implement the neoliberal policy package.

Given the dominant view that domestic factors were primarily responsible for the economic crisis, political elites did not unite against a common foreign

Table 2.1   Key economic indicators in the five countries

	Indonesia	South Korea	Thailand	Malaysia	Philippines
Annual GDP growth rate (%)					
1995	8.2	8.9	8.9	9.8	4.7
1996	7.8	6.8	5.9	10.0	5.8
1997	4.7	5.0	−1.7	7.3	5.2
1998	−13.0	−6.7	−10.2	−7.4	−0.5
1999	0.3	10.7	4.2	5.6	3.2
Private consumption expenditure growth rate (%)					
1995	12.6	9.6	7.6	11.7	3.8
1996	10.9	7.1	6.8	6.9	4.6
1997	6.7	3.5	−1.1	4.3	5.0
1998	−3.3	−11.4	−12.3	−10.8	3.4
1999	0.5	10.3	2.9	3.1	2.6
Inflation rate (%)					
1995	9.4	4.4	5.7	4.1	8.0
1996	8.0	4.9	5.8	3.5	9.0
1997	6.2	4.4	5.6	2.7	5.9
1998	58.4	7.5	8.1	5.3	9.7
1999	20.5	0.8	0.3	2.7	6.7
Unemployment rate (%)					
1995	7.2	2.0	1.1	2.8	8.4
1996	4.9	2.0	1.1	2.5	7.4
1997	4.7	2.6	0.9	2.6	7.9
1998	5.5	6.8	4.4	3.2	9.6
1999	6.4	6.3	4.2	3.4	9.4
Three–month interbank lending rate, end of month (quarterly average, %)					
97 4Q	23.2	n.a.	20.8	n.a.	26.5
98 1Q	34.2	23.5*	24.5	n.a.	20.6
98 2Q	40.0	18.3	22.0	11.1	17.4
98 3Q	55.9	10.7	13.0	9.3	16.7
98 4Q	48.6	7.6	7.9	6.7	15.5
99 1Q	39.6	6.7	6.0	6.2	14.4
99 2Q	27.6	5.7	5.0	3.5	10.3

Table 2.1 (Continued)

	Indonesia	South Korea	Thailand	Malaysia	Philippines
Monthly average stock price index (quarterly average, June 1997 = 100)					
97 3Q	89.5	94.8	114.2	83.7	85.4
97 4Q	63.5	65.7	85.7	60.4	67.1
98 1Q	67.4	73.8	91.3	60.0	72.2
98 2Q	63.8	54.3	70.0	51.6	72.7
98 3Q	55.7	46.1	47.5	34.8	50.9
98 4Q	50.8	63.8	64.7	42.6	60.2
99 1Q	57.1	83.1	70.0	50.8	71.2
Fiscal balance as % of GDP					
1995	2.2	0.3	3.2	0.8	0.6
1996	1.2	0.1	0.9	0.7	0.3
1997	−0.7	−1.3	−0.3	2.4	0.1
1998	−2.3	−4.4	−2.8	−1.8	−1.9
1999	n.a.	n.a.	−3.5	n.a.	−3.7

Source: The Asian Recovery Information Center, http://aric.adb.org.
^aThe figure is the average of January and February only.

enemy. Instead, some domestic institutions and actors became the targets for blame. Other domestic actors belonged to the camp that was responsible for implementing the neoliberal policies, behind which the IMF and other international creditors stood firm. Large parts of the mass publics suffered from these neoliberal reforms, while the immediate and main beneficiary of them was foreign capital. All this made a solid consensus about the neoliberal policies difficult to maintain among key policymakers and even more difficult to impose on the seriously affected mass publics.

Depending on precrisis political conflicts and elite configurations and on how the crisis divided political elites over neoliberal reform packages, political developments in the crisis-hit countries were likely to take different paths. The next chapter deals with the precrisis political conflicts and elite configurations.

3 Political circumstances before the Asian economic crisis: elite configurations in the five countries

This chapter surveys the prior political circumstances of the five countries in East and Southeast Asia whose foreign currencies were hardest hit in the 1997–8 crisis as discussed in Chapter 2: Indonesia, South Korea, Thailand, Malaysia, and the Philippines. I focus, in particular, on their elite configurations, driven by my thesis, in Chapter 1, that the chances of a consensual political elite forming during a crisis depend in part on the elite type that existed before a crisis. For this purpose, I follow Higley and Burton in distinguishing four ideal types of elites according to the extent of their integration and differentiation (Table 1.1).[1] The four types are labeled ideocratic, consensual, fragmented, and divided. Basically, these labels denote different modes of elite behavior and structure that result from the number of elite groups and their relations with each other.

Indonesia

Suharto's New Order regime rested on a divided elite configuration composed of dominant military elites and their civilian allies on the one side and repressed and weak civilian counter-elites on the other. There was a highly unbalanced power relation between the two camps. This unbalanced relation stemmed primarily from the decimation or complete destruction of communist and left-oriented nationalist forces when the New Order regime was established in 1965. The New Order regime developed in the wake of an authoritarian-populist regime headed by Sukarno. The New Order regime, dominated by the military, transformed the old Sukarno order. It destroyed the leftist forces centered in the oldest communist party in Asia, the PKI (Partai Komunis Indonesia). At the same time, it co-opted noncommunist civilian forces by purging uncooperative leaders from their ranks.

After an ostensibly pro-Sukarno military coup on September 30, 1965 failed in two days, counter-coup forces led by General Suharto launched a massive and bloody purge of leftists in the military and in the wider society.

Arrests were made of most PKI leaders and cadres. Antara news agency and communist-controlled newspapers and magazines were banned. A number of universities that had come under excessive influence of the PKI were shut down. The powerful PKI-affiliated students union, Consentrasi Gerakan

Mahasiswa Indonesia (CGMI), too was banned. The large number of representatives of the PKI and its affiliated bodies were denied their status as members of the MPRS [the People's Consultative Assembly – Interim]. Within a short period of time, the PKI and all its affiliated organizations were totally eliminated.[2]

This destruction of communist organizations was accompanied by widespread killings of communists and pro-Sukarno nationalists, numbering perhaps half a million lives.[3]

General Suharto not only got rid of the leftists but also transformed the old fragmented elite. The first postcolonial parliamentary election in 1955 had produced 28 parties in parliament. The four largest parties together accounted for 78 percent of the total vote: PNI (Indonesian Nationalist Party), Masjumi (Consultative Council of Indonesian Moslems), Nahdlatul Ulama (Ulama Association), and PKI. They won 22.3, 20.9, 18.4, and 16.4 percents of the national vote, respectively. Six smaller political parties, including the Catholic, Christian, and Socialist parties, won between 2.9 percent and 1.3 percent of the vote. All other parties won less than one percent of the national vote.[4]

This highly fragmented party system was forcibly restructured by Suharto's victorious forces. By 1973, all of the old surviving political parties had been forced to merge into two new parties. Islamic parties were forced to join the new United Development Party (PPP) under the leadership of Idham Chalid, a former leader of Nahdlatul Ulama. All former nationalist parties, including PNI and the two Christian parties, were forced into the new Indonesian Democratic Party (PDI).[5] The PPP and PDI thus constituted a new party system, along with the previously reorganized Golkar, which had long existed as an umbrella organization of social associations but underwent a major structural change in 1967, two years after Suharto's victory. Golkar still maintained its nominal status as a nonparty entity, but it now functioned, in effect, as the governing party.[6]

The two nongovernment parties, PPP and PDI, together won from 38 percent to 25 percent of the total vote in parliamentary elections that were held periodically during the New Order. Voters were given a limited range of choices in these elections, and the elections were never free of government manipulations. The effective number of parties in terms of votes was 2.09 in 1977, 2.01 in 1982, 1.74 in 1987, 1.94 in 1992, and 1.66 in 1997.[7] Thus, the New Order regime brought the fragmented party system to a halt and, at once, debilitated political parties in parliament to the extent that they were active only during election periods.

Even if the conflict between powerful governing elites and suppressed counterelites was not as visible as in other divided elite configurations, such as under Marcos in the Philippines,[8] some extra-parliamentary opposition groups were still noticeable. One was the "Petition of 50," an anticommunist and reformist group led by the marine Lieutenant General Ali Sadikin. Another was the Democratic Forum, led by Abdurrahman Wahid, the chairperson of Nahdlatul Ulama. Two professional politicians were also prominent opponents of Suharto's regime. One was Sri Bintang Pamungkas, a former PPP member, who was later imprisoned.

The other was Megawati Soekarnoputri, Sukarno's daughter, who was elected PDI leader despite the regime's effort to block her election in 1993. She was forcibly deposed as party leader in June 1996 because of her potential threat to President Suharto's reelection. As in other Asian military regimes, such as South Korea's, Indonesian students were vociferous in their opposition to the New Order regime, especially in 1974 and 1978, when massive demonstrations against the regime took place.[9]

Unlike its Thai counterpart, the Indonesian military, which was the backbone of Suharto's regime, displayed relatively little internal factionalism that threatened its command structure and Suharto's presidency. By the mid-1970s, Suharto had filled all important military positions with "personal loyalists and officers who could not possibly mount a challenge to [him]."[10] Until the late 1980s, observers of the Indonesian military could not identify conflicting military factions – only at most, diverging tendencies and attitudes. Writing in 1990, for example, Harold Crouch distinguished between "the generation of military leaders who had fought in the revolution against the Dutch in the late 1940s" and "post-revolutionary officers who have graduated from the military academy at Magelang or equivalent institutions since 1960," among whom he found differing attitudes about the military's future political role.[11]

Some dissenting military factions in the government camp, however, began to appear during the late 1980s and early 1990s. During this period, more attention was paid to the influence of what was called the army's Murdani wing, that is, General Benny Murdani and his group of officers. Once Suharto's most dedicated loyalist, Murdani was appointed to the highest position in the armed forces even though he had been "an intelligence specialist who has never personally commanded any unit larger than a battalion."[12] But his relationship with Suharto became strained because of his attempts to interfere in the first family's business affairs. Murdani was replaced as armed forces commander by General Try Sutrisno in 1988, though he still held the position of commander of Koptamtib (the Operational Command for Restoration of Security and Order). Murdani's replacement was in part a preemptive move by Suharto to get Lieutenant General Sudharmono elected as vice president. Murdani was then appointed Minister of Defense, but without any power in military affairs. He retired from public life when Suharto was reelected as president in 1993. The group around Murdani, a Roman Catholic and an alleged supporter of Megawati, together with a massive reorganization of the armed forces that included the promotion of General Feisal Tanjung, a devout Muslim, as armed forces commander,[13] appeared to lay the basis for a serious military division between "a 'red and white' group (*golongan merah putih*, the colors of the national flag, symbolizing the unity of a multi-religious, multi-ethnic nation)" and "a 'green group' (*golongan hijau*, symbolizing Islam)."[14] Yet, it is probably accurate to say that, despite the existence of some critical active and retired military officers, Suharto was still in control of the military until his sudden resignation in May 1998.[15]

The relative invisibility and weakness of opposition groups in the New Order regime resulted not only from the repressive state apparatus but also from the country's sound economic performance. This economic success is summarized as follows:

> By the mid-1960s many informed observers despaired of any prospect of significant economic advance .... Yet little more than a decade later Indonesia was being hailed as one of Asia's success stories. Economists cite Indonesia from 1966 to 1968 as one of the most swift and effective instances of inflation control in the twentieth century. By the late 1980s Indonesia was being classified among the select group of developing countries destined shortly to become newly-industrialized economies, following the successful path of Asia's outward-looking industrial economies. President Soeharto has received international awards in recognition of the country's success in food production and family planning. Once the world's largest importer of rice, Indonesia achieved self-sufficiency in this crop in the mid-1980s .... Later in the decade, the country attracted international attention for its continuing success in poverty alleviation, even during the period of painful macroeconomic stabilization occasioned by a halving of world oil prices.[16]

In sum, the New Order military regime forcibly transformed the fragmented elite configuration of the Sukarno years into a more clearly dichotomous and divided configuration, with the balance of power skewed sharply toward those in control of the economically successful and authoritarian regime. In other words, the Indonesian New Order regime successfully replaced previous elite fragmentation by forcibly eliminating extremist parties and seriously truncating elite conflicts. Yet, these conflicts continued under the surface, and a highly unbalanced power relation existed between a strong government and a weak opposition before the 1997 crisis.

Thailand

The Thai political elite before the crisis can best be described as fragmented, even if a lingering military–civilian conflict implied that Thai elites bordered on divided. Political power was scattered among several military factions, newly civilianized political factions, and wholly civilian factions, with the king attempting to mediate among the many contending elite groups.

First, in the last precrisis general election in November 1996, ten political parties succeeded in gaining parliamentary seats, with the largest party obtaining 31.8 percent of the seats. The effective number of political parties in parliament was 4.32.[17] In addition to the comparatively large number of lower house parties, the Senate, whose membership was equal to two-thirds of the lower house members, formed another significant political power center, even if it became increasingly weak.[18]

Active military officers, cautious enough not to explicitly engage in politics after their political debacle in 1992, formed another powerful force. This force itself was ridden by factional conflicts, however. The best known faction was the

Young Turks, that is, the Young Military Officers Group. They were led by Class Seven, – the 1960 graduates of the Chulachomklao Royal Military Academy – and had been involved in several coup attempts, particularly during the 1980s. Notable leaders were then Colonel Manoon Roopkachorn and Colonel Prachak Sawangchit. Former Major General Chamlong Srimuang was also a leader of the Class Seven faction. Their chief rival faction was Class Five – the 1958 graduates of the same Military Academy. General Suchinda Kraprayoon who led the coup against the administration of Prime Minister Chatichai Choonhavan in February 1991 had been president of Class Five in the Military Academy. Another clear faction called themselves Democratic Soldiers and presented themselves as sophisticates who espoused a version of state socialism. The core of the Democratic Soldiers was Class Five at the Army Preparatory School. The Democratic Soldiers had been affiliated with the Thai People's Party or Puang Chon Caho Thai, which, however, had lost its political identity by September 1992. General Arthit Kamlangek was leader of Thai People's Party. General Chavalit Yongchaiyudh, a Class One member of the Royal Military Academy and founder of the New Aspiration Party, was said to be associated with the Democratic Soldiers faction. In the military factionalism that was mostly based on graduating classes, other classes were also notable, in particular, Classes 8, 9, and 12 of the Royal Military Academy, even though they were much less cohesive.[19]

The extensive elite fragmentation in Thailand grew out of inconclusive but somewhat restrained struggles for power between the many military and civilian groups that emerged after the absolute monarchy's curtailment in 1932. These struggles were somewhat restrained in the sense that almost all the major confrontations in Thailand did not involve serious elite casualties, even if a significant number of political activists, including politically active students, were killed during several mass revolts and coups, especially during the 1970s and the early 1990s.

There were two indicators of the restrained character of these elite power struggles. The first was how coup plotters, including their leaders, were treated in a series of unsuccessful coups. The second was how the targets of successful military coups were dealt with. Concerning the first indicator, the Young Turks initially supported the Prem Tinsulanonda government (1980–8), but later they launched an unsuccessful coup against it in April 1981. The 38 coup plotters, whose leader was Colonel Manoon, were dismissed from the Army. Colonel Manoon then led another failed coup four years later. On that occasion, he was allowed to go into exile as part of a deal to avert further bloodshed. A year later, 28 of the 38 Young Turks officers were "reinstated to active service; Colonel Manoon officially remained a fugitive from prosecution."[20] But before the 1991 coup, "Chatichai allowed him [Manoon] back into the country from exile, arranged his promotion from colonel to major-general and then took him under his wing in the Defense Ministry."[21] Having successfully escaped a concerted manhunt by the 1991 coup junta, Manoon came back to work as chief adviser to Interior Minister Sanan in the second Chuan Leekpai government that took office in 1997 amid the economic crisis.[22]

Similarly, General Arthit was one of the major targets of the 1991 coup, along with Prime Minister Chatichai and Manoon. One reason for the coup was that General Arthit, Deputy Prime Minister in the first Chatichai coalition government and leader of Thai People's Party, had been appointed to "the additional post of Deputy Defense Minister with some control over the budget and promotions."[23] General Arthit had played a key role in thwarting the 1981 Young Turks coup. He was arrested and detained in the successful 1991 coup. A month later, however, he was released from detention and allowed to go abroad. More important, from my point of view, in January 1992, one year after the coup, Arthit resigned from Thai People's Party and joined Sammakhi Tham (literally, meaning Unity in Virtue), the political party which was set up by the key figures in the 1991 coup junta.[24] In short, the line between political comrades and opponents in the military was too fine and too shifting to be of any lasting significance in Thailand. While political events were shaped heavily by jockeying for place within the military, this jockeying seldom had fatal, or even permanent, consequences.

The restrained elite conflict was also reflected in the bloated number of generals in the Thai army. "Independent estimates by military analysts range from 700-1000, or as many as one general for every 300 troopers." This meant that there were more generals than tanks (the army has about 720 tanks).[25] As the class size of military academy cadets, ranging from 150 to 200, was by comparison not very large, the large number of generals was obviously the result of accommodative (or inclusionary) promotions in the army.[26]

In conclusion, before the economic crisis, the Thai elite was quite badly fragmented, although its internal conflicts were comparatively restrained. There was no anti-system party as such. However, the military still remained a threat to Thailand's democratic stability. As I will explain in more detail in Chapter 5, the political cleavages remained very fluid. The ever-shifting party membership and party coalitions characterized the political party system.

The Philippines

The precrisis Philippine elite configuration was formed after the demise of the divided elite configuration under Marcos's sultanistic regime. The new configuration was characterized by the extensive fragmentation among the dominant oligarchic elites, flanked by two weak anti-system political parties, though elite infighting was less restrained than in Thailand.

The Philippines has been and still is collectively ruled by a number of landed and other oligarchic elite families, except during Marcos's predatory sultanistic or single-man rule, even though nontraditional political groups increasingly strengthened before the crisis.

> Estimated to comprise not more than 120 families, these per-martial law elites controlled not less than 60 percent of the national income. The prominent elites of the country included: the Laurel, Cojuangco, Imperial, Nepmuceno. Quirino and Crisologo families in Luzon; the Osmena, Cuenco,

Lopez, Araneta, Durano, Montelibano Roxas and Ayala clans in the Visayas; and the Alemndras, Florendo, Pelaez, Dimaporo and Tamano clans in Mindanao.[27]

More specifically, former President Corazon Aquino herself belonged to one of the traditionally powerful landed families. This fact in part accounted for her sluggish land reform, over which the national elites were severely divided.[28] "She was born . . . into the extremely wealthy land owning Cojuangco family from Tarlac Province [in fact, the wealthiest family in the province]." Her husband, Benigno Aquino, who "was regarded as the politician most likely to succeed Marcos" unless the latter declared martial law in 1972, was also "born into an elite landowning family from Tarlac Province."[29] Eduardo Cojuangco, who is a cousin of Corazon Aquino and a 1992 presidential candidate, belonged to a different branch of the Cojuangco family. Imelda Marcos was born "to an impoverished branch of the wealthy Romualdez family from Leyte in the central Visayan Islands."[30] Even if Marcos himself was not born to any traditionally powerful family, his family turned out to be another powerful family later. President Ramos was a cousin of former president Marcos but later switched his political royalty to the Corazon Aquino group, in contrary to what Eduardo Cojuangco did. Salvador H. Laurel, who gave up his initial bid for presidency on behalf of Corazon Aquino and instead ran for vice-presidency in 1986 and presidency in 1992, came from one of the traditionally powerful families, "the son of wartime President and later Senator Jose B. Laurel."[31] From this perspective, the powerful Catholic Church is itself one of the great landed or business groups.

Even if it may be true that "state power, recaptured by the landed elites after 1986, was significantly reduced by the expansion of the political clout of businessmen, professionals and entrepreneurs," the dominant position of traditionally powerful families was undeniable in Philippine politics before the crisis. Of 201 House Representatives in 1987, 164 were from "decades-old oligarchic families and political clans"; and so were 145 of 201 in 1992.[32] Even the reduced number in 1992 was still striking, given a 1987 constitutional article that

one-half of the seats allocated to party-list representatives [that is, of up to 50 seats] shall be filled ... by selection or election from the labor, peasant, urban poor, indigenous cultural communities, women, youth, and such other sectors as may be provided by law, except the religious sector

for the first three terms.[33] It is also not certain that the above 1992 figure included those newly formed landed elites and self-transformed ones. It should be noted that many old landed elites transformed themselves into industrial or financial elites; as well, there were newly rising landed elites whose origins did not go back to pre-Marcos era.[34]

These collectively dominant oligarchic elites were divided into several contending camps in the 1992 presidential election. There were seven contending candidates including Miriam Defensor Santiago who championed reform of the oligarch-dominated establishment. The winner, Fidel Ramos, received only 23.6 percent of the national vote. The vote proportions received by defeated candidates were: Miriam Defensor Santiago 19.7 percent, Eduardo Cojuangco Jr 18.2 percent, Ramon V. Mitra 14.6 percent, Imelda Romualdez Marcos 10.3 percent, Jovito R. Salonga 10.2 percent, and Salvador H. Laurel 3.4 percent.[35] The effective number of candidates was 5.84. This great number of presidential candidates (or, alternatively, political parties in the presidential election) was all the more striking because of the downsizing effect of pure and simple plurality rule employed in the presidential election.

The great number of presidential parties did not take two anti-system political forces, Muslim separatists and communists, into account. Both had challenged the elite establishment through violent uprisings. But the threat from the communists had abated significantly by the early 1990s because of the installation of democratic government and the end of the Cold War. The establishment of democratic government dissipated the movement's revolutionary thrust. So did the closure of all US military bases, especially Clark Air Base and Subic Bay Naval Base, by November 1992, which had lost their strategic importance with the Cold War's end.

By 1985, CPP [Communist Party of the Philippines] influence nationally was estimated at 33 percent [of the 41,400 barangays or barrios, the smallest administrative unit], with the NPA [New People's Army] in control of at least 12 percent of the barangays.[36]

A self-estimate by the NPA was that during the same period, when its strength was at the peak, it had 30,000 troops and 10,000 barrios were under its influence.[37] Yet, by the mid-1990s, the number of NPA guerrillas had shrunk to as few as 7,000,[38] and in July 1992, President Ramos asked the legislature to legalize the Communist Party. The Philippine government and Communists were engaged in peace negotiations before the outbreak of the 1997 crisis, even though no conclusion had been reached.

The divided Muslim movement, which was confined to the southern parts of the Philippines, was also losing strength. "Originally the stronger of the two guerrilla armies [that is, Muslim separatists and the communists], Moro forces had dwindled by 1986 to one-third their original size."[39] By 1992, the movement had divided into three main groups: the largest was Moro National Liberation Front (MNLF); the second was its 1978 splinter group, Moro Islamic Liberation Front (MILF); and Abu Sayyaf was the smallest but most militant group reported to be active after 1992. Notably, the government reached a peace agreement with the MNLF in September 1996.[40] This called for establishing an autonomous regional council that would be replaced by a freely elected permanent body in 1999.

Under the agreement Misauri [the MNLF leader] stood for election as governor of the Autonomous Region of Muslim Mindanao encompassing the four provinces (Sulu, the Tawi Tawi island group, and the mainland provinces of Maguindanao and Lanao del Sur) then controlled by the MNLF; after three years a referendum would be held to determine if the remaining provinces referenced in the 1976 Tripoli Accord should be added to the Autonomous Region. It was also specified that 7,500 of the MNLF's 16,000-member military would be incorporated into the national army and police.[41]

However, the two more militant bodies, MILF and Abu Sayyaf, both of which sought full independence and an Islamic state, rejected the agreement.

In addition to the declining yet still active communist and Muslim anti-regime forces, the military was once a threat to the post-Marcos democratic regime, even though the Philippine military has never been dominant over the civilian sector. The military played a significant role in bringing down Marcos's repressive civilian regime. The divided elite configuration under Marcos's predatory rule came to an end, only after the dissatisfied military wing mounted an anti-Marcos coup and gained the support of the masses, the Catholic Church and parts of the business sector.[42] After the democratic transition, which was a joint action of anti-Marcos military and civilian political forces, there were several attempts by the military to gain political hegemony over the civilians. The anti-Marcos military forces felt that "Aquino was unfaithful to the largely unwritten agreement .... Instead of her agreement to give the military a larger role in the government to make changes, regarding cronies, etcetera, there was betrayal," even though "they [the anti-Marcos military forces] felt that they had caused the collapse of the Marcos regime and his flight to Honolulu."[43] Yet, all of the military coups between 1986 and 1989 failed.[44] This is contrasted with Thailand. In Thailand, absolute monarchy came to an end in 1932 as a concerted action between the military and civilian camps, like the case of Marcos's sultanistic regime; however, in due course, the military camp got the upper hand over the civilian camp.

The aforementioned decline of the communist and Muslim anti-system forces reinforced the dominance of the civilian sector over the military by lessening the need for military repression and promoting peaceful bargaining efforts in dealing with the antiregime forces. At the same time, however, civilian elite groups felt less pressured to build a unified front against their common enemy.

In sum, the Philippine elite configuration before the crisis featured a large number of oligarchic elite groups that faced two weakening antisystem forces, the Communists and Muslim separatists. The existence of still active Communists demonstrates that the Philippine elite did not have solid consensus on property rights, which was also reflected in violent land reform controversies. The continuing armed struggle of Muslim separatists shows that the Philippines did not even complete nation-state building. The dominant and disintegrated oligarchic elites did not have consensus on another constitutional issue, term limits for elected officials including presidents. I leave this constitutional issue for Chapter 5 because the issue became salient at the onset of the economic crisis. In the chapter, I will also show that the collectively dominant fragmented oligarchic elites had narrow popular support bases and failed to mobilize voters along a linear political cleavage dimension.

Malaysia

The Malaysian elite configuration could be described as semi-consensual: elite integration was strong, while elite differentiation was not sufficiently wide. Malaysia's ruling alliance, based in the National Front, consisted of civilian parties that were comparatively well organized and not conspicuously personalistic. By obtaining 65.05 percent of the votes in the 1995 general elections, the ruling National Front (Barisan Nasional) won 162 of the 192 parliamentary seats, which was far beyond the two-thirds of parliamentary votes required to amend the constitution. The effective number of parliamentary parties was 1.39. This was the smallest among the five countries, even smaller than that of the Indonesian military regime.[45] This implies that the elite differentiation was quite narrow.

The foremost characteristic of the National Front was that it was based on sectional organizations within the Malay, Chinese, and Indian ethnic communities. It originated in a functional division of political and economic labor, although the original format of this division of labor was later significantly modified. In the original format, however, the Malay elite controlled the government, the Chinese elite, capital, and the Indian elite, labor.

Concerning the historical origins of Malaysia's ethnic politics, it is notable that the ethnic coalition was part of the British colonial legacy and not the outcome of violent inter-elite conflicts.[46] For about 100 years, the British colonial government had ruled Malaysia with the collaboration of ethnic Chinese in business and ethnic Malays in government, while importing Indian labor to Malaysia. Most Malay people remained in the agricultural sector.

> The British found it convenient to use the established Malay leadership in local administration. A Malayan administrative service was formed as a junior partner of the Malayan Civil Service, founded in 1906. A conscious effort was made to create an administrative class from the traditional elite, which would work with the British. Through the early part of the twentieth century, British policy ... accorded the Malays a pre-eminent position in government .... By the last quarter of the nineteenth century large numbers of Chinese started coming into Malaya lured by the prospects of plentiful employment on the estates and mines. Immigration, in its early stages, was unrestricted and not subject to controls. In the case of the Indian immigrants the British followed a conscious policy of encouraging Indian labor in order to offset the Chinese.[47]
>
> The British 'protected' the Malays, giving a pre-eminent position in government and administrative employment. The Indians, primarily, worked on the estates, while the Chinese were allowed a free hand to set up business.[48]

From my point of view, it is important to emphasize that the Alliance, the original formula of power-sharing, was not an outcome of (or a measure to cope with) any persistent and violent interethnic conflict *per se* or *an elite settlement*. Rather, the most serious interethnic clash in Malaysia, that is, the 1969 communal riots, took place long *after* the establishment of the Alliance, and the event forced the Alliance to modify its original formula of power-sharing.[49] Even if the Alliance or its successor, the Barisan Nasional (National Front), is also sometimes discussed as a case of consociationalism and consociationalism is considered as a solution to serious ethnic conflict, it should be also noted that the Malaysian consociationalism did not come out of any prior serious experience of interethnic conflict.

After Malaysia's peaceful independence from British colonial rule, the ethnic division of labor was maintained. The reasons were that the ethnic Chinese dominated the economy, the Malay political elite needed their help to manage the newly independent national economy, and also the Chinese numerical strength, about 30 percent of the total population, could not be ignored. Next to Singapore, which was part of Malaysia until 1965, Malaysia has the largest ethnic Chinese community in Southeast Asia in terms of proportion to the country's total population.[50]

Despite the political salience of ethnic cleavages in Malaysia, its ethnic elite groups were functionally complementary to each other. This was because each elite group controlled a different strategic sector in society. This functionally complementary elite condominium was distinct from most ethnic elite configurations in other countries that are largely based on regions and thus lack functional interdependence. In a functionally noncomplementary alignment, none of the ethnic elites makes an exclusive claim over capital or labor or service sector, but each ethnic elite controls some part of every sector. This means that ethnic conflict is likely to be more severe or violent because there is intense competition for dominance within and between the sections.

As the elite groups were arrayed along ethnic or community lines but were functionally complementary to each other in Malaysia, there was not much room or need for the military to act as an independent force. As late as the mid-1960s when Malaysia was involved in armed confrontation with Indonesia over newly incorporated colonies of Sarawak and Sabah, it relied heavily on British armed forces for its national defense. This was also true in its early confrontation with communists. As of 1994, the total armed forces were 114,500 men strong, which was 0.6 percent of the total population.[51] It is striking that Malaysia is one of the few Third World countries that have never experienced a military coup. There is not much space for ideological forces to seek a place in the elite condominium, either. The suppression of communist insurgency was almost completed early in the Malaysian state building or by 1960.

By the time of the economic crisis in 1997, the condominium had been in power for more than three decades, even though it was challenged by a bloody clash between pro-Alliance and anti-Alliance forces in 1969 and had been threatened by defections from the pivotal Malay party, UMNO (United Malay National Organization) during the 1980s and 1990s.[52] Consequently, Malaysia exhibited the most integrated and generally consensual elite among the five countries at the outbreak of the economic crisis. However, unlike other consensual elite configurations, it had a small number of effective parties, less than two. This meant that structural differentiation among the elite groups was not wide, nor was electoral competition very meaningful. The ruling coalition was above the constitution and not bound by constitutional stipulations, due to its predominant power position. In sum, the Malaysian elite configuration was closer to the consensual type of elite than any of the other types. Yet, compared to any other regular consensual elite configurations, it was not differentiated enough. Consequently, it is perhaps best to classify it as semi-consensual.

South Korea

South Korea's precrisis elite configuration emerged in 1987 when the governing party suddenly succumbed to the opposition's demands without any reservation. This democratic transition did not begin as a consequence of direct negotiation between the authoritarian and democratic camps. In fact, one of the opposition leaders, Kim Young Sam, rejected the government's offer to have a talk. Nonetheless, the Korean transition had many features of negotiated transition. Hence, Samuel Huntington identified the 1987 transition as a transplacement, and Michael Burton and Jai P. Ryu concluded that it was an elite settlement.[53] Both government and opposition camps claimed the greater credit for initiating the democratic transition. The ambiguity involved in the democratic initiation permitted the once authoritarian ruler, Roh Tae Woo, to claim that he was a true democrat. This meant that the sharp political division between authoritarian and democratic camps started to abate, if still salient, as early as 1987.[54]

In the 1987 presidential election, the oppositions failed to unite against the presidential candidate of the military regime. As a result, the authoritarian/democratic cleavage was crosscut by new regional divisions. This cleavage structure set the subsequent political course. In the largely four-way contest, there were two authoritarian candidates (Roh and Kim Jong Pil), and two democratic candidates (Kim Young Sam and Kim Dae Jung). Roh, Kim Young Sam, Kim Dae Jung, and Kim Jong Pil represented the northern and southern parts of the southeast region (Kyongsang), the southwest region (Cholla), and the mid-central region (Chungchong), respectively. Roh won 36.6 percent of the votes, Kim Young Sam 28 percent, Kim Dae Jung 27.1 percent, and Kim Jong Pil, 8.1 percent.[55] Thus, South Korea's democracy began with moderately fragmented elites (Figure 3.1). Yet, its elite fragmentation was much less extensive than in Thailand and the Philippines. This was reflected in the relatively smaller number of political groups in the 1987 presidential election: the effective number of candidates was 3.41.

After the divided democratic camp's defeat in the presidential election and the ruling party's failure to secure a majority of parliamentary seats the next year, Roh and two Kims excluding Kim Dae Jung created a supermajority party, the Democratic Liberal Party (DLP), in January 1990. This merger was basically a

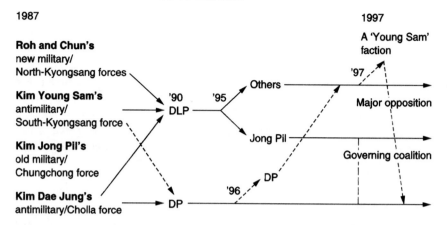

Figure 3.1 Parties and party alliances in Korea after 1987.

Note: The figure does not include Chung Ju Young's party that contested the 1992 parliamentary and presidential elections. This party was not permanent unlike other political groups that originated in 1987. The unbroken lines stand for the main streams regardless of party names. DP in the figure represents the Democratic Party and Chun refers to Chun Doo Hwan.

subversive collusion among the top leaders that was aimed at changing the presidential system to a parliamentary system.[56] It displayed further erosion of the democratic/anti-democratic cleavage among the elites. The former authoritarian camp was willing to take the chance of losing executive power to Kim Young Sam, who, in turn, did not hesitate to get his democratic reputation tainted by joining forces with the former authoritarian groups. The collusion, which did not have any solid popular basis, turned out unsuccessful by 1992. In the March 1992 parliamentary election, voters basically disproved it. The previously supermajority party in parliament only obtained 38.5 percent of the total vote and failed to secure even a majority of seats, which was a crucial blow to any constitutional amendment move.[57]

In the 1992 presidential election, Roh and Kim Jong Pil stood by Kim Young Sam, despite some serious disagreements among them. Taking advantage of the immense campaign resources and organizations under the control of the governing party, Kim Young Sam won 42 percent. Kim Dae Jung obtained 33.8 percent, which included the swing votes that disproved Kim Young Sam's reconciliation with the former military camp.[58] Even though his election was, to some extent, attributable to the governing party and its former military-turned factions, Kim Young Sam kept a distance from the former military groups and emphasized his civilian roots, once elected. He initially enjoyed the unprecedented popularity that no one could challenge. In particular, Kim Dae Jung announced political retirement after his second consecutive defeat. Roh and Chun Doo Hwan had been deeply divided since Chun's self-imposed exile after Roh's apparent reluctance to defend his former colleague during his term. President Kim first purged politicized top army officers by fiat. In 1993, he also shocked people by introducing a system of real-name banking transactions without much consultation, and, consequently, purged a significant number of corrupt politicians who were tied to the former authoritarian regime. In 1996, after his initial hesitation, Kim also brought Chun and Roh as well as their army colleagues before the court for their roles in the 1979 mutiny and 1980 Kwangju Incident and for their illegal fund raising. The indictment, imprisonment, and pardon of the two prominent former military men signaled the eventual disappearance of the so-far salient military/anti-military division.

While the democratic/anti-democratic (or military/anti-military) cleavage gradually receded, the other salient political cleavage in the 1987 transitional election, that is, regional divisions, remained unchallenged. As with other ascriptive cleavages, the strength of regional attachments did not much fluctuate over time, and there had been no serious crisis that could demolish voters' regional attachments. The voters that came from the largest and second largest regions, Kyongsang and Cholla, whose combined population accounts for somewhere between 50 percent and 70 percent of the total population, tended to show strongest regional attachment in their voting.[59] Voters that came from Chungchong showed a moderate extent of regional attachment. Voters whose birthplace was Seoul, Kyonggi, Kangwon, Cheju, or North Korea were least affected by regional attachments. In the 1992 presidential election, according to a survey,[60] 87 percent of the voters who originally came from Kim Dae Jung's stronghold, Cholla, regardless of their current places of residence, voted for him. This was responsible for 62 percent of his total vote in the election. Meanwhile, 65 percent of the voters who came from Kim Young Sam's stronghold, Kyongsang, voted for him. This accounted for 49 percent of his total vote.

This ascriptive voting was less responsive to election campaigning and thus was rigid over time. This was especially true of Kim Dae Jung and his supporters. The same survey showed that 96 percent of the Kim Dae Jung supporters from Cholla in 1987 stood by him in 1992. By contrast, 65 percent of his 1987 supporters from the other regions voted for him in 1992. As for Kim Young Sam, 68 percent of his supporters from Kyongsang in 1987 cast their ballots for him in 1992, while 53 percent of his supporters from the other regions in 1987 voted for him in 1992.

Of course, the rigidity and magnitude of regional voting in Korea was not as grave as those of ethnic voting in Malaysia. However, right before the onset of the Asian economic crisis, the apparent dominance of regional political divisions and the voting *en bloc* by regionally attached voters made otherwise extensive elite differentiation only limited. Like the ethnic voting in Malaysia, the rigid voting patterns of regional voters reduced the magnitude of democratic uncertainty and had the effect of raising the entry barrier to free electoral competition, even though South Korean elections were freer and more uncertain.

Another problem with regional voting was that it was policy-neutral. In other words, regional mandates did not provide presidents any guidance in making socioeconomic policies. Nor did such presidents carry a strong electoral mandate to pursue any controversial economic policy. Consequently, no president had been given a certified democratic mandate to settle the conflicting claims by opposing interests. As a result, the government's policies about any controversial

Table 3.1 Concentration of economic power in Korea: Chaebols' assets as a proportion of national assets before the crisis

	1994	1995	1996	1997
Top five chaebols	23.39	25.42	26.98	29.92
Top ten chaebols	32.42	33.87	35.64	36.29
Top 30 chaebols	41.56	44.86	46.61	46.25

Source: Seung No Choi, *Big Businesses in Korea, 1999* (in Korean) (Seoul: Free Enterprise Center, 1999), 23.

issue oscillated widely, depending on volatile public whims or sentiments.[61] This meant that the Korean government was very weak in implementing public policies, and it also signaled that there was no elite consensus about socioeconomic policy measures. From another perspective, the prevalence of policy-neutral regional voting meant that presidents were given virtually carte blanche to pursue any economic or social policies, and, consequently, it was no wonder that South Korean democracy showed some features of delegative democracy including the seemingly imperial president.

Along with the rigid regional cleavages, the concentration of wealth in a few industrial oligarchs had the effect of blocking extensive elite differentiation. Although political dictatorship ended in 1987, economic monopoly or oligopoly was sustained or rather strengthened, as seen in Table 3.1. The top five big business families accounted for 30 percent of the national assets right before the economic crisis, and the top 30 took about 46 percent.

One may think that the economic concentration in Korea is nothing peculiar but rather a universal phenomenon observed in industrialized societies and in Asia's rapid economic growth through close business–government ties. Inhak Hwang contends that economic concentration is not a Korea-specific phenomenon; in fact, the multiple-index-based economic concentration in Korea remains much lower, compared to other OECD (Organization for Economic Cooperation and Development) economies.[62] However, when we focus specifically on the assets-based index of economic concentration, Korea indeed came out on top among the OECD countries. In addition, after surveying the economic concentration in Indonesia, Korea, Malaysia, and Thailand, Stephan Haggard concludes that the economic concentration in Korea remains rather either lower or not noticeably higher than in the three other Asian economies.[63] Nonetheless, chaebols or Korean industrial business groups are unique in the sense that their scope of business is so extensive that it includes irrelevant sectors, even though they are not *financial* holding companies.

This concentration of economic power not only blocked extensive economic differentiation and allowed chaebol owners to exert arbitrary power over other non-chaebol businesses, but it also had the effect of curbing political differentiation by narrowing the financial sources of political parties or, alternatively, by raising the entry barrier to free electoral competition.[64]

In sum, after decades of authoritarian rule, South Korea transited to democracy in 1987 when the former authoritarian camp accepted the opposition's democratic demands without any reservation. The transition was not preceded by a direct elite negotiation over transition terms. Yet, the former authoritarian camp still maintained significant power during the transition and successfully got its candidate elected president. After joining forces with a former democratic leader in 1990 and helping to get him eventually elected president two years later, the former military group was gradually divested of power until the issue of cleaning authoritarian legacies virtually disappeared in 1996. Fortunately, South Korea was no longer troubled by the authoritarian/democratic cleavage when it was hit by the Asian economic crisis.

Despite the successful resolution of the military's political involvement and consequently the gradual, complete disappearance of military threat to democracy, no Korean elites were habituated to the existing rules of the game. They had not developed consensus about concrete economic policies and had never seriously contested elections with important socioeconomic issues. Instead, the existing political groups were divided by the rigid regional cleavages, and elections were characterized by rigid voting and not substantially open to policy-oriented parties. This feature of closed election was most conspicuous in Kim Dae Jung's regional supporters, which accounted for about 20 percent of the electorate. In addition to the rigidity of voting and the consequent concentration of political power in regionally based leaders, the concentration of wealth in a few industrial business families made the elites short of sufficient differentiation. All these considerations lead me to conclude that the Korean elite was not fully consensual.

Conclusion

I have now summarized the precrisis elite configurations in the five countries that were most seriously affected by the 1997–8 economic crisis. This summary is necessary because of my assumption, in Chapter 1, that the chances of a consensual political elite forming during a crisis depend in part on the elite type that existed before a crisis. Table 3.2 displays the elite types in the five countries before the economic crisis. Indonesia alone had a divide elite. Thailand and the Philippines had clearly fragmented elites. Although the South Korean elite type remained ambiguous, I would classify it as semi-consensual, along with the Malaysian elite, primarily because its extent of differentiation was limited.

Concerning Indonesia, I noted that the balance of power was highly uneven between the regime elites and counter-elites. Owing to the New Order regime's sound economic performance, as well as its repressive nature, the opposition elites were weak. Internal divisions among the regime elites were not conspicuous, either. This power imbalance in Indonesia was important, because, as I posited in Chapter 1, a divided elite is likely to pursue an elite settlement only if the balance of power is more or less even at the outset of a crisis.

Table 3.2 Elite configurations in precrisis Asia

	Elite	
	Integration	*Differentiation*

Consensual
  South Korea
  Malaysia
  (both semi-consensual)
	Strong	Wide

Ideocratic No case	Strong	Narrow

Fragmented
  Thailand
  The Philippines
	Weak	Wide

Divided Indonesia	Weak	Narrow

In the cases of two-fragmented political elites, I did not much discuss why they were fragmented or which political cleavages were prevalent among them. These questions will be addressed in Chapter 5 that deals with the two fragmented national elites.

Given the classification of political elites in the five countries, my main questions are (1) whether postcrisis Indonesia might nevertheless pursue an elite settlement, (2) whether the two fragmented elites will overcome or reduce their fragmentation through a convergence following the crisis, and (3) whether Malaysia's semi-consensual elite as well as South Korea's will maintain or deepen its somewhat precarious elite consensus as a consequence of the crisis. Chapters 4–6 deal successively with each of these questions.

4 Economic crisis, divided elites, and prospects for an elite settlement

In Chapter 1, I hypothesized that a crisis may trigger the transformation of divided elites via a settlement, if no grossly uneven distribution of power exists between major elite groups before the crisis. My hypothesis can be restated as follows: an economic crisis may result in an elite settlement where there are a *small* number of political elite groups that engage in *severe* and *inconclusive* elite conflicts. There are, in fact, three independent variables in this hypothesis: the number of political elite groups, the severity of precrisis conflict, and the precrisis balance of elite power.

Among these variables, severe conflict and a small number of conflicting groups imply a divided elite whereas an even power balance among the groups implies a possible elite settlement. Clearly, not all divided elite configurations lead to elite settlements because the crucial power balance necessary for a settlement is often absent. Even where power is balanced, moreover, a settlement may require the absence of other obstacles such as weak leadership, strong external interventions, and major crosscutting ethnic conflicts.

With the above three variables in mind, I will now examine the Indonesian case. As seen in Chapter 3, Indonesia was the only one of the five countries studied here that satisfied the basic precondition for an elite settlement, namely, the existence of a divided elite before the Asian economic crisis. However, the balance of power between government and opposition elites was highly skewed in favor of the former. Consequently, my prediction must be that the crisis could not trigger an elite settlement in Indonesia. In fact, this was what happened, with the Indonesian elite fragmenting instead.

Precrisis power imbalance, external pressures, and no elite settlement

As seen in Chapter 3, Suharto had been too powerful to challenge before the crisis. Yet, the power imbalance began to shift after the onset of the economic crisis. A series of heavy foreign pressures seriously undercut Suharto's executive power. Consequently, only two months after his seventh and unanimous election as president, he unexpectedly resigned. The fact that Suharto's sudden resignation was much leveraged by the IMF and creditor countries meant that none of the weakly organized opposition groups was ready to govern even if they were very vocal, whereas the old governing elite groups remained very powerful during the subsequent democratic transition. The opposition groups could not aggregate their interests and negotiate terms of the transition with the old regime camp. The process of institutional design for the post-Suharto era was also led by the government and by old-regime opposition forces such as PPP (United Development Party) and PDI (Indonesian Democratic Party) in the Suharto-era parliament. As a result of no settlement between regime and opposition elites, Indonesia not just left the old rules of the game essentially intact, but also many key political issues were left unanswered. The unsettled basic political issues as well as a proportional representation system in the 1999 general election facilitated excessive proliferation of political groups and the consequent resurgence of fragmented political elites.

After the ill-considered imposition of the IMF's first economic policy package for Indonesia failed to control the growing economic crisis and instead aggravated it during the last two months of 1997, the previously limited effects of the crisis rapidly spread through the society. Specifically, "the IMF directive to close down 16 insolvent banks caused panic, precipitating a run on two-thirds of the country's banks, further weakening the financial sector and eroding faith in the economy."[1] Feeling threatened, Suharto began to back away from economic liberalization, which had been the thrust of his relatively autonomous economic policymaking team including Central Bank Governor Soedradjad Djiwandono and Finance Minister Marie Muhammad. Suharto adopted cautious stance, which was reflected in the budget he announced on January 6, 1998 that included an increase in government spending and subsidies to fuel and major staples. Additionally, "he created the Financial and Economic Stabilization Board and placed Fuad Bawazier, then Director of Taxation in the Department of Finance, in a position higher than that of his boss, Marie Muhammad."[2]

However, the IMF and the US government were strongly opposed to the more cautious budget and successfully pressured Suharto to remove state subsidies to staples, fuel, and electricity, a mere nine days after his budget was announced. Consequently, Suharto's governing power was sharply weakened. However, before the subsidies were fully removed, and amid a major outflow of capital and a further fall in the rupiah's value, Suharto attempted another "deviant" measure, that is, the establishment of a currency board in early February. This was a desperate attempt to stabilize the rupiah. Despite the heated debate that this action created, Suharto was unanimously reelected to presidency, with Bacharudin J. Habibie elected as vice president, four weeks later. Suharto immediately appointed personal associates, including his daughter, to the new cabinet.

After ten Japanese banks refused to reschedule Indonesia's private debt and advised Vice President Habibie to stick to the IMF bailout package on his first visit abroad after the election, in late March,[3] the Indonesian government was forced to sign yet another agreement with the IMF in early April. Under this agreement, the government promised to carry out its agreements with the IMF *to the letter.* The currency board proposal was not discussed, but the IMF allowed Indonesia to continue subsidizing rice and soybeans for an indefinite period. Subsidies to other foodstuffs, medical materials, animal feed and energy were to be phased out and ended by October.[4] Once again, Suharto backed away from his preferred policy and lost the tug of war with the IMF. His governing power eroded further.

Entering May 1998, the Indonesian government announced sharp increases in fuel and energy prices and public transport fares.[5] These increases pushed up the already surging rate of inflation and drove the discontented public to express their anger in massive anti-Chinese street riots and student-led anti-government demonstrations that turned increasingly bloody. The riots and demonstrations claimed six lives in Medan, North Sumatra, on May 5. They spread to Jakarta, despite warnings of the military (ABRI), by May 8, and four students were shot near Trisakti University on May 12. The violent rioting, looting, and arson claimed more than 500 lives during the following two days.[6]

Suharto returned to Jakarta, cutting short a visit to Egypt, and implied that he might step down. The next day, however, he denied any intention to resign and instead proposed a cabinet reshuffle. In response, students occupied the parliament and renewed their demonstrations and demands for his resignation. On May 19, Suharto announced that he would step down only after holding new elections. Yet, on May 21, one day after US Secretary of State Madeleine Albright called on him to provide for a democratic transition by resigning, together with other opposition and government figures' calls for his resignation, Suharto abruptly resigned and transferred presidential power to Habibie.[7] Thus, a democratic transition began under the leadership of an interim figure, who had been Suharto's trusted associate.[8]

Because Suharto's resignation occurred suddenly, domestic counter-elites were only poorly prepared to take initiatives in the new political opening. The weak and disorganized opposition camp did not contemplate negotiating terms of the transition with the old regime camp. Major opposition figures sat together only after student groups arranged a roundtable for them and practically forced them to attend it in November 1998. While some student groups engaged in actions that opposed a special session of the MPR (Majelis Permusyawaratan Rakyat or the People's Consultative Assembly), others focused on setting up a presidium to oversee a transitional government and prepare for a general election. Toward this end, they contacted each of the five prominent potential opposition leaders who had refused to participate in the government-led special MPR session: Abdurrahman Wahid, Megawati Soekarnoputri, Amien Rais, Sri Sultan Hamengkubuwono X, and plus Bishop Belo. None of these leaders liked the idea of a presidium, however, and Bishop Belo did not attend the meeting. Instead of creating a presidium, the four leaders who did attend reached a so-called "Ciganjur Agreement." Yet, their demands were moderate and, to a significant extent, ambiguous. The agreement included, among others, upholding national unity while decentralizing the government, ending Habibie's transitional government with a democratic election, eliminating the military's political intervention gradually over six years, and investigating Suharto's wealth according to the laws.[9] Subsequent behavior and statements by the four leaders soon showed that the agreement had little meaning.

The agreement also had no significant influence on the special MPR session.[10] It was notable that the Ciganjur leaders did not explicitly address the biggest current issue, which was the legitimacy of the special MPR session. This was an important omission, because some student groups had already planned or taken actions that rejected the special session, making violent clashes imminent. Only two days after the Ciganjur agreement, a peaceful mass action was countered with a flurry of shots.[11] Nonetheless, the Ciganjur meeting was important because it brought major opposition leaders together to discuss the crisis for the first time.

Parallel with the Ciganjur meeting of the opposition leaders and a People's Special Session at the Proclamation Monument compound held by radical students, the government-led special MPR session unfolded. The MPR had 1000 elected and appointed members. In addition to 500 DPR (the House of Representatives or Dewan Perwakilan Rakyat) members including 75 nonelected military members, there were 100 functional (or social) group delegates and 149 provincial delegates. The remaining 251 seats were bonus seats that were proportionally allotted to four DPR political groups. The former president, Suharto, appointed all of these 500 non-DPR members in the MPR.[12]

The old-regime MPR special session, on November 13, decided to keep the ABRI represented in the MPR/DPR and DPRD I and II (Regional Houses of Representatives – provincial and local levels) and reduce its parliamentary membership by stages.[13] The government-dominated MPR session also adopted a new electoral system. The government and Golkar, having abundant funds and nationwide organizations, at first preferred a district-centered electoral system but later shifted to a proportional representation (PR) system based on small districts. At the other extreme, the PPP faction wanted a PR system based on large districts or provinces, considering an uneven power balance that favored the governing party. It worried that if electoral districts became smaller, "from the 314 regencies/municipalities in whole Indonesia, 260 of them [would] only fight for one seat which w[ould] certainly be won by Golkar."[14] The PPP proposal, ironically, was the same as the existing system under the Suharto regime. The electoral system that was finally agreed to was fundamentally a list PR system incorporating some district-system features: DPR members were to be elected proportionally according to a quota/largest-remainder system in separate elections in each of the 27 provinces.

Significantly, no new extra-parliamentary opposition forces, such as Partai Demokrasi Indonesia-Perjuangan (PDI-P) led by Megawati, Partai Kebangkitan Bangsa (PKB) founded by Abdurrahman Wahid, and Partai Amanat Nasional (PAN) led by Amien Rais, participated in the institutional design. However, they did not sabotage the process or reject any MPR decisions either. The Indonesian democratic transition was in this respect characterized by cautious or moderate positions among new opposition or "reformasi" forces, apart from vocal student groups. There was no explicit bargaining that occurred between the regime and opposition forces, even though the new opposition groups undeniably exerted some influence on the government. The cautious stances of new opposition groups and the lack of explicit bargaining between the two camps stood in sharp contrast to the radicalism in the streets and in the public more generally.

No settlement between regime and new opposition elites means that Indonesia not just left the old rules of the game essentially intact, but also many key political issues were left unanswered. For instance, even though the general election was perceived as the first round of a presidential election scheduled for November 1999, there was no explicit rule on how to elect president. The only consensus was that a new Indonesian president was to be elected indirectly in an MPR general session in November 1999. However, the 1998 special MPR session did not rule on details about presidential election. In fact, the detailed presidential election rules were set just one day before the presidential election in the 1999 MPR session.[15]

In addition to the ambiguous presidential election rules, there was no elite agreement on many other important rules or issues, so that each elite group could take an issue with them later when they did not turn out favorably. Among questions that had no clear answers were as follows:

1   whether a woman could be elected president,
2   how the two hundred regional and social group representatives to the MPR were to be chosen,
3   whether military officers were to be included in the regional representatives to the MPR in addition to their 38 reserved DPR/MPR seats,
4   whether the positions of head of state and head of government could be separated without constitutional revision,
5   whether the state should be secular,
6   whether the state should be unitary or federal,
7   how to deal with separatisms in outlying regions such as East Timor.

The open-ended rules and unsettled issues allowed the political elite to maintain its ambiguous, indecisive, but also sometimes intransigent attitudes. Indonesian political elites preferred to leave any controversial issues untouched and let circumstances unfold instead of actively trying to control those circumstances. These indecisive attitudes were also fostered by other institutional features such as the indirect election of president. The MPR's indirect election of president, which was basically equivalent to a multiround election system with PR in the first round and majority rule in the second round, did not have a strong filtering effect. Had there been, instead, a popular presidential election by plurality rule, in which minor political parties play little or no role, the number of viable parties would have been much smaller.[16] This new electoral system would also have made the wait-and-see attitudes among political leaders too risky and costly, and thus have facilitated a broad preelection coalition among them, expectedly between Megawati and Wahid.

Strong old-regime forces and disunited opposition forces: political cleavages in the 1999 general election

The general election in June 1999 was not a showdown between clearly competing old-regime and opposition forces. This was largely due to the weak position of the opposition camp and its internal disunity. By January 1999, more than 160 political parties had emerged. Forty-eight of them, however, contested the DPR election. To participate, parties had to have executive boards in at least nine (out of 27) provinces, and in half of the municipalities and districts in each province.[17] But 48 parties did in fact meet these requirements. Of those 48 parties, 21 obtained at least one seat in the DPR. Six parties succeeded in obtaining at least ten DPR seats, which was required for political parties to stand again at the next elections. The effective number of DPR parties in terms of seats was 5.24, including the nonelective military/police faction.[18] The complete election results were as follows: of 500 DPR seats, PDI-P took 153 with 34 percent of the popular vote; Golkar, 120 with 22 percent; PKB, 51 with 13 percent; PPP, 58 with 11 percent; PAN, 34 with 7 percent; PBB (Crescent Star Party), 13 with 2 percent; and others, 33 with 11 percent, in addition to ABRI's 38 unelected seats.

In the general election, a disorganized or poorly coordinated opposition camp contested elections, whose rules were set by the still powerful old-regime forces. Three major opposition parties, PKB, PAN, and PDI-P were not united against the two old-regime parties, Golkar and PPP.[19] In addition to the preexisting old-regime versus reform cleavage, which was intensified by the economic crisis, the contending political parties were divided between nationalism and Islam. Political Islam had been suppressed under the New Order regime and yet revived rapidly after the regime collapsed. Many would-be political groups, which had not yet developed their own independent political networks before the Asian economic crisis, used relatively intact religious organizations as their political foundations when the system became suddenly opened.

The nationalism versus Islam line pitted the mainly nationalist or secular Golkar and PDI-P against the largely Islamic or at least Muslim-based PKB, PAN, and PPP parties, even though none of these parties was homogenous in its composition.[20] This cleavage line is inferred from a notable difference in electoral performance between PDI-P and Golkar, on the one hand, and PKB, PAN, and PPP, on the other. Electoral supports for PDI-P and Golkar were *nationwide*, while supports for the other three parties were *more regionalized*. Figure 4.1 pictures the percentage of votes that each party obtained in the 26 electoral districts that spread from the country's western to eastern end, excluding East Timor. The figure shows that only the two largest parties, PDI-P and Golkar, had nationwide support; in contrast, the other parties failed to obtain a significant vote, that is, at least ten percent across all or most electoral districts. PDI-P obtained more than ten percent in every district except South Sulawesi, the home of Habibie. Golkar won more than 10 percent in all districts. Even Bali, the home of Megawati, cast 10.38 percent of its vote for Golkar.

On the other hand, votes for the third most popular party, PKB, were largely concentrated in the middle region, Java, which is the most heavily populated

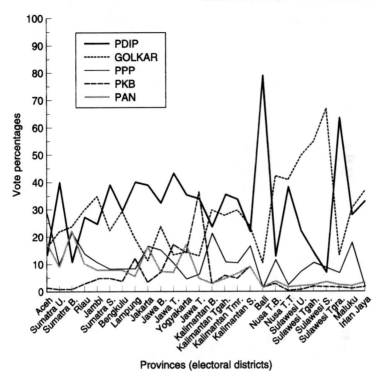

Figure 4.1 Political parties' vote percentages from west to east in Indonesia.
Source: National Election Commission (Indonesia).

region. The votes for the two other Muslim-based parties, PPP and PAN, did not spread out over the country either. Their support rates gradually decreased from west to east; their modal support rates were located in Aceh and West Sumatra, respectively. Thus, even though PPP was in fact led by a traditional Muslim and PAN was formally a catch-all party, PPP and PAN were more successful in the western regions, where modernist Islam is relatively strong, and PKB's support came predominantly from the central region, where traditional Islam is relatively strong.

Correlation analysis of the parties' support rates in electoral districts in Table 4.1 supports the hypothesis that the above-mentioned nationalist versus Islamic cleavage line was crosscut by a cleavage between adherents of the old regime and anti-regime reformers. Correlation analysis confirms Golkar's anti-reform position: its votes were negatively correlated with votes for all three major reformist parties, PDI-P, PAN, and PKB while the negative correlation between the two old-regime parties was not only small but also statistically insignificant.

Meanwhile, based on Table 4.1, it is not easy to identify the position of PPP on the reform cleavage line, because the vote correlations between PPP and the three reformist political parties were not consistent. The correlation between PPP and

Table 4.1 Correlations between political parties' vote percentages in the
26 electoral districts in Indonesia

	PDI-P	Golkar	PPP	PKB	PAN
PDI-P	1.0	−0.61[**]	−0.54[**]	0.12	−0.27
Golkar		1.0	−0.13	−0.41[*]	−0.42[*]
PPP			1.0	−0.19	0.52[**]
PKB				1.0	0.04
PAN					1.0

[**] Significant at 0.01 level (two-tailed).
[*] Significant at 0.05 level (two-tailed).
Source: National Election Commission (Indonesia).

PDI-P votes was −0.54, which was statistically significant. However, the vote correlation between PPP and PKB or PAN was statistically insignificant or positive. This implies that voters considered PPP primarily as an Islamic party rather than as an old-regime party.

Nonetheless, PPP was indeed an old-regime party. We can find this in the party's exceptional performance in the nonwestern regions, compared to other Islamic or Muslim-based parties. Figure 4.1 shows that votes for PAN and PPP were closely correlated, especially in the country's western parts; yet, this correlation disappeared further eastwards. In the eastern areas, only PPP among the three Islamic or Muslim-based parties succeeded in obtaining significant votes, though its performance there was much weaker than in the western areas. This was primarily due to the fact that PPP, unlike PAN and PKB, had long participated in elections held by the old regime.

In addition to the two most salient crosscutting cleavages, two lesser cleavages also fostered elite fragmentation. These were regional attachments and Islamic sectarianism. Figure 4.1 shows that two major parties scored a landslide victory in their respective strongholds. The Golkar's support rate exceeded 65 percent in South Sulawesi, whereas PDI-P obtained more than 80 percent of the Bali votes. This implies that regional attachments to a political party or its leader also influenced the election outcomes, even if this influence was more marginal compared with the two main cleavage dimensions. Sectarianism within Islam is another political cleavage that contributed to elite fragmentation. Even though Indonesia boasts the largest Muslim population in the world, only about 30 percent of its 180 million Muslims are deeply religious; these Muslims tend to think that Islam should have a significant political role. The rest majority of Muslims, however, are only nominally religious; they are less likely to believe that their religious belief requires them to vote for a particular political party, and they are able to separate political from religious spheres. There were four notable Muslim groups: (1) the 40,000-member Indonesian Muslim Intellectuals (ICMI) that was closely linked to President Habibie, (2) "the 28-million-member Muslim charitable and educational organization Muhammadiyah (Way of Muhammad)" that represented modernist (i.e., less vulgarized) and more politicized Islam and had been led by Amien Rais, (3) "the 30-million-strong Nahdlatul Ulama (Awakening of the Ulamas)" that stood for traditionalist (i.e., more vulgarized) and more tolerant Islam and was headed by Abdurrahman Wahid, and (4) a variety of student/ex-student groups including the 250,000-member Indonesian Muslim Students Association, which would rather keep some distance from political parties.[21] We may add PPP-affiliated Islamic groups to this list. Islamic sectarianism accounted for the fact that so many Islamic groups contested the general election under this or that Islamic banner.

In sum, when the authoritarian political system was suddenly opened largely due to foreign pressures, many of the potential opposition groups that had not been strongly organized under the old regime used religious organizations as their political foundations. Although Suharto resigned, the dominant old-regime groups still remained intact, so that the legacy of authoritarianism was very strong. Consequently, the Indonesian elite was not only divided between Islamists and nationalists but also between old-regime supporters and reformers. These cleavages, supplemented by other two lesser cleavages, regional ties and Islamic sectionalism, made fragmented national elite reemerge three decades after the violent military coup quelled the fragmented elite of the Sukarno years. Yet, the two notable former anti-regime parties, the Communists and militant Islamists, did not reemerge. When compared with the Sukarno era, the range of political fragmentation was narrower in terms of the number of contending political elite groups and their internal dissensions. Islamic groups were still politicized but less violent. The old Communist versus anti-Communist cleavage was replaced by a more moderate cleavage between old-regime supporters and reformers. Nonetheless, the new extensive fragmentation was sufficient to give disproportional bargaining power to small parties and bring about captured presidency and policy immobilism.

Logrolling, veto power, and captured presidency: an outcome of elite fragmentation

Given the extensive political party fragmentation, the crucial presidential election could go one way or another, depending on what minor elite groups did. I now want to show how the largest plurality winner in the general election, PDI-P, lost virtually all major national posts, and what I call "captured presidency" came into being.

After the regrouping of 21 DPR parties, ABRI (or TNI/POLRI), and two additional MPR groups of regional and social group representatives, eleven "factions" or parliamentary negotiation groups were formed in the MPR.[22] The distribution of 695 MPR seats among factions, with the number of DPR seats in parentheses, was as follows: 185(153) seats for PDI-P, 183(120) for Golkar, 69(58) for PPP, 57(51) for PKB, 48(41) for Reformasi, 14(13) for PBB, 5(5) for PDKB, 14(12) for KKI, 9(9) for PDU, 38(38) for TNI/POLRI, and 73(0) for UG (Social Groups).[23] These fragmented parliamentary groups, most of which in turn

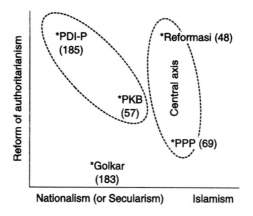

Figure 4.2 Elite alignments in the MPR general session.

were loosely bonded assemblies of different subgroups, were responsible for electing a president during the general MPR session extending from October 1 to 21, 1999. As the largest vote-getter, PDI-P, accounted for only 27 percent of the total MPR seats, far shorter of simple majority, there was no guarantee that the party would take the presidency. This uncertainty earlier drove four small Islamic party leaders, Amien Rais, PBB (Crescent Star Party) Chairperson Yusril Ihza Mahendra, PKU (Muslim Community Awakening Party) Chairperson Yusuf Hasyim and PPP Chairperson Hamzah Haz to construct a loose voting bloc, called the Central Axis, including other minor Islamic parties. Figure 4.2 shows the initial alignments at the opening general session of the MPR with the number of MPR seats in parentheses. To win any MPR election, it was necessary for the largest plurality party, PDI-P, to block a strategic alliance between Golkar and the Central Axis while maintaining its strategic alliance with PKB. Blocking the Golkar-Central Axis alliance required the vertical cleavage line of Figure 4.2 to remain more salient than the horizontal line. For the sake of simplicity, I assume that other minor parties or voting blocs, including the military, would remain either neutral or mixed in their final voting or offset each other's voting.

To see why PDI-P lost the presidency to an alliance of minor parties, it is necessary to look at MPR elections before the presidential election through which strategic alliance between Golkar and parties in the Central Axis gradually and accidentally developed via logrolling. The first election was the election of MPR chairperson on October 3, in which Amien Rais was elected against the PKB/PDI-P coalition's candidate, Matori Abdul Djalil, the PKB chairperson. Amien Rais had not been on the projected list of candidates, until one day before the election. Close competition was expected between Abdurrahman Wahid and Golkar's Akbar Tandjung. However, the actual competition turned out to be between Reformasi's Amien Rais and PKB's Matori. Surprisingly enough, the social group faction, to which Wahid belonged, did not nominate him as its MPR chairperson candidate. PKB could not nominate Wahid because he was not a PKB faction member. It instead nominated Matori. To take advantage of this opportunity, the Reformasi faction withdrew its nominee, A. M. Fatwa, and subsequently, Amien Rais entered the race with Wahid's endorsement. Consequently, the major voting cleavage line was drawn between PDI-P and a nationalistic PKB group on the one hand and Reformasi, PPP, and other Central Axis groups on the other hand, while Golkar strategically stood behind the Islamic Central Axis. The outcome was the Central Axis coalition's victory by 305 votes to 279. The other candidates nominated by PPP, PDI-P, Golkar, PBB, and Military/Police were marginalized in the race.[24]

Subsequently, Golkar Chairperson Akbar Tandjung was elected DPR speaker in return for his earlier support for Amien Rais in the MPR chairperson election. His election was not opposed by PDI-P either, which now realized that it would need some support from Golkar to win the presidential election in the end. He secured 411 votes against the runner-up, PDI-P candidate, Soetarjo Soerjogoeritno, who obtained only 54 votes. This was the second consecutive defeat on the part of PDI-P.

This growing alliance through logrolling between Golkar and the Central Axis threatened the likelihood that Megawati would be elected president. The coming presidential election was the first presidential election by vote in Indonesia's history. As noted earlier, the election rule was set just one day before the election day, October 20. It was absolute majority rule in which they would hold an unlimited number of ballots until one candidate won an absolute majority.[25]

At first, the presidential race was believed to be a largely three-way competition among PDI-P's Megawati, Golkar's Habibie, and the Central Axis's Wahid. This meant that two cleavage lines could crosscut each other: one between nationalist Megawati and anti-Megawati forces, and the other between authoritarian Habibie and anti-Habibie forces. Along one cleavage line, Islam versus nationalism, Habibie took the center, while Wahid was located in the middle of the reformist versus authoritarian line. This meant that none of the three candidates would win an absolute majority in the first round. They would have to go to a second round, where Megawati and Habibie would be candidates. If the second round was dominated by the reform cleavage line, Megawati would be the winner in the end. By contrast, if the nationalist/Islamic cleavage turned out to be dominant, Megawati's victory would be unlikely. If the two cleavages carried relatively equal weights, the winner remained highly unpredictable, given that many MPR factions were not internally cohesive.

This expectedly complex game became rather simplified when Habibie withdrew his candidacy at the last minute. Subsequently, the presidential race became a two-player game with the nationalist/Islamic cleavage line being dominant. Habibie had been under heavy pressure to quit his candidacy due to his aides' involvement in the Bank Bali scandal and his narrowly consulted decision to offer East Timor the option of independence. His government's moves to dismiss the corruption charges against Suharto and his youngest son, Hutomo "Tommy" Mandala Putra at the last minute further narrowed his support base. Habibie's hand-picked vice presidential candidate, Wiranto, two days before election day, announced that he would not enter the electoral fray. All of these together contributed to Habibie's accountability speech being rejected on the presidential election day: 355 MPR members rejected his speech while 322 accepted. This final blow to Habibie's presidential bid forced him to withdraw his candidacy early in the morning. After searching alternative venues, Golkar finally decided to vote for Wahid.[26]

Once the common enemy of all democratic or reform forces, whether Islamic or nationalistic, stayed out of the presidential race, the winner was Wahid. He was closer to the median along the Islamic/nationalist cleavage line in the MPR. He won 373 votes while Megawati got 313, with five abstentions. He was supported by Reformasi, PBB, PPP, and Golkar, even though not all of these party/faction members voted for him. Notably, he was also supported by PKB, which had thus far vowed to support Megawati despite Abdurrahman Wahid's bid for presidency.[27] PKB "shifted its support to Abdurrahman, but PKB chairperson Matori Abdul Djalil and some party executives continue[d] to support Megawati."[28]

To calm down the riots by Megawati's frustrated supporters, she was nominated as vice presidential candidate by PKB. She could defeat PPP's Hamzah Haz 396 to 284 only after Wiranto and Golkar's Akbar Tandjung withdrew their candidacies along with PKB's strong lobby for her candidacy and Amien Rais's support. [29] Local presses called this victory her consolation prize.[30]

In sum, Islamic or Muslim-oriented parties including PAN and PPP, collectively called the Central Axis, maneuvered so successfully that the largest plurality winner in the general election, PDI-P, lost virtually all major national posts and had to remain satisfied with what was called a consolation prize, vice presidency. The first runner-up in the general election, Golkar, took the position of house speaker in return for its earlier support for Amien Rais, the Central Axis's MPR chairperson candidate. This logrolling between Golkar and the Central Axis later helped them to get the PDI-P presidential candidate, Megawati, defeated, when Golkar's presidential candidate, Habibie, withdrew his candidacy on election day. The Central Axis also drove PKB, the second runner-up in the general election, into a difficult position by nominating Abdurrahman Wahid, as its presidential candidate. Although PKB was founded by Wahid, its leadership had vowed to support Megawati as presidential candidate right until before election day. Wahid, characterized by awfully ambivalent attitudes, joined the MPR as a social group representative. At the last minute, the PKB members except its chairperson and some party executives changed their minds to desert Megawati. Consequently, Wahid was elected president with the strategic support of numerous small Islamic parties, over which he had little political influence. PKB, which he himself helped to get founded, remained split over his bid for the presidency. Thus, a captured or weak president came into being: no single party was strongly committed to him, and any political party was positioned to exercise veto power. Moreover, Wahid's election was based on the strategically manipulated salience of nationalism/Islamic cleavage. This fact meant that he had yet to build consensus on major socioeconomic issues, which were, to a greater extent, in line with the old-regime/reform cleavage. Not only all major national positions but also the first cabinet posts were dispersed widely to fragmented elite groups. The cabinet was officially called the "national unity" cabinet, but it was sometimes and more properly dubbed as a "rainbow cabinet."[31] An immediate outcome would be policy immobilism.

Conclusion

In Chapter 1, I asserted that economic crisis promotes political cooperation only if the balance of power among political elite groups is even at the onset of the crisis. In other words, economic crisis is sometimes conducive to political consensus building and, consequently, democratic stability. However, this positive effect of economic crisis on democratic stability holds good only if the balance of power among conflicting elite groups is not skewed highly in favor of a particular elite group. More specifically, I argued that previously divided elites undergo an elite settlement, one of the most outright manifestations of political cooperation, during a crisis only if the balance of power among the divided elite groups is even at the onset of the crisis.

In this chapter, I have illustrated my argument, using the case of Indonesia during the Asian economic crisis. As my theory predicted, the path to stable democracy through an elite settlement was not taken in Indonesia, where there was no approximately equal balance of power among the precrisis divided political elites. Suharto resigned only after much foreign pressure was imposed on his presidency. There was no direct bargaining between the dominant regime and the weak and disorganized opposition forces. Power was simply transferred to Suharto's trustees who exercised much influence over the whole process of power transfer to a democratically elected government. In particular, the rules of the game were designed by the largely Suharto-era MPR forces. The old electoral system and other political rules were not much overhauled and remained ambiguous. The two old regime parties including the governing Golkar survived and turned out to be the second and third largest political parties in terms of MPR seats. A new democratic regime was finally born, but it was located largely in the old regime incubator.

The Indonesian democratic transition ended in a fragmented elite configuration. During the transition, indecisive and opportunistic actors played under ambiguous and open-ended rules of the game, without any attempt to make an elite settlement. This game resulted in a political system that lacked a clear- or a strong-mandated leadership and that gave small and mid-size political parties disproportionate power including veto power. A democratic transition without any outright confrontation or settlement among the elite groups meant that Indonesia would continue to be troubled by the task of cleaning up authoritarian legacies after the transition. Much more worrisome was the birth of a captured president, which would be followed by policy immobilism.

The next chapter takes up the question of whether fragmented elites become consensual elites in the wake of economic crisis. I use the cases of the Philippines and Thailand.

5 Economic crisis, fragmented elites, and prospects for elite convergence

This chapter discusses the prospects for an accommodation among fragmented elites amidst the Asian economic crisis. As argued in Chapter 1, the route to consensus among fragmented elites is via elite convergence. The core element of a convergence is that, stimulated by a crisis, part of a previously fragmented elite forms a single stable electoral coalition or bloc powerful enough to threaten semi-loyal or anti-system elite groups with virtually permanent exclusion from executive power. My hypothesis is that the formation of such a stable dominant electoral bloc, which may over time contribute to a narrowing of critical differences, is more likely to occur when there is a dominant linear political cleavage line that has a nonarbitrary center, like a left–right ideology line.

In Chapter 3, I observed that two countries, the Philippines and Thailand, displayed fragmented elite configurations at the onset of the Asian crisis. Elite fragmentation and the holding of democratic political elections are the initial conditions necessary for elite convergence. In this chapter, I deal with Filipino and Thai political cleavage structures before the crisis to determine whether there was a dominant political cleavage along which the fragmented elites were arrayed and, if so, whether it was linear. This is followed by the discussion of the prospects for elite convergence.

Political cleavages before the crisis

Thailand: No predominant political cleavage

A remarkable feature of Thailand's fragmented elite configuration before the crisis is that two of the most widely discussed political cleavages in comparative politics, class-based ideology and ethnic identity, did not account for the Thai configuration at all. To understand the structure of political cleavages and their origin in Thailand, we need to attend to factional conflicts within the dominant military camp. Most Thai political groups originated primarily in the collectively dominant but internally fragmented military camp, even though the political influence of *serving* military officers was significantly curtailed by increasing pressures for military professionalism after the bloody crackdown on anti-military demonstrations in May 1992. But the military, including retired military officers, had collectively dominated the weak civilian sector throughout modern Thai history. This collectively dominant military camp was the basis on which most of the precrisis Thai political groups were founded.

Most Thai elite groups and political institutions during the 1990s had some sort of military tie. Most conspicuously, the Senate was controlled by military officers until 1996. In the late 1980s, "up to 85 percent of the Senate membership was drawn from the armed forces and the police."[1] As late as March 1996, serving and retired military officers constituted a significant minority in the much weakened Senate. As *Straits Times* reported in March of that year,

> Among the 260 names announced [note that all senators were appointed], only 39 are active-duty military officers, including the chiefs of the three armed forces and the supreme commander. Another 13 are retired officers. Together, they account for only one-fifth of the new Senate. In the previous 270-member Senate, one-third of the senators were active-duty military officers. If retired officers were also taken into account, the military occupied more than half the seats in the upper house.[2]

The military also maintained ties with most political parties in the House of Representatives. Above all, the Thai Nation Party (or Chart Thai) was the most notable military-backed party or *pak taharn,* and it consisted of several factions. It was initially led by retired Major General Pramarn Adireksan and included a substantial number of military figures among its active members. The National Development Party (or Chart Pattana) was formed in 1992 by retired Major General and former Prime Minister, Chatichai Choonhavan, who had earlier led the Chart Thai Party in the 1988 national election. Similarly, the New Aspiration Party was organized by former army commander Chavalit Yongchaiyudh who served as General Chatichai's Defense Minister. Still again, the Righteous Force or Palang Dharma was formed by former Major General and Bangkok Governor, Chamlong Srimuang. Even the Democrat Party, which is the oldest party in Thailand and known for its antimilitary position, selected retired Major General Sanan Khachornprasart as its Secretary General to replace Veera Musikapong, whose faction had been backed by a wealthy Bangkok business person, in 1987.[3] General Sanan held that position until early 2000 while also leading a military-tied faction within the party, parallel with a mostly civilian faction that was led by Prime Minister Chuan Leekpai. Thus, as late as November 1998, *the Far Eastern Economic Review* reported that "He [Sanan] has linked himself with officers of Chulachomklao Military Academy's Class 7.... The leader of those two abortive coups [in 1981 and 1985], Maj.-Gen. Manoon Roopkachorn, is now his chief adviser at the Interior Ministry."[4] Another general, Harn Linanond, had been deputy leader of the Democrat Party in 1985. He was a former commander of the Fourth Army Region, but he quit the army in a dispute with General Arthit Kamlangek in 1984, who was in turn one of Harn's pre-cadet Class Five members and then army commander in chief and supreme commander of the armed forces.[5] The Social Action Party, a 1974 offshoot party of the Democrat

Party, was more conservative than its parent group. It was one of the "devilish" parties that supported the Suchinda government in April 1992, which collapsed during the May 1992 mass demonstrations in Bangkok.[6]

Neither class-based ideology nor ethnic identity played any significant role in this military-rooted factionalism. This is attributable, in part, to the relatively mild experience of the Cold War and communist threat. It is also attributable to Thailand's lack of a colonial experience and the divisive legacies that it creates, such as privileged ethnic groups. Thailand is the only country in Asia that did not experience colonialism or foreign military occupation in its modern history. This reduced communism's appeal in Thailand because Asian communism gained much of its appeal through struggles for national liberation. Communist forces in Thailand were the most divided, and thus the weakest, among the five countries considered here, even though Thailand could not avoid fallout from the Vietnam War and undertook military actions against communists in Laos.[7]

No experience of foreign occupation, in particular, no Western colonialism, also meant that Thailand had not experienced the typical colonial policy of "divide and rule," and, consequently, ethnic conflicts kept a low profile compared with other Southeast Asian countries, despite economic dominance by ethnic Chinese in Thailand as elsewhere.[8] Before significant industrial development got underway, ethnic Chinese were well integrated into Thai national life. Thus, a historian of the Chinese in Thailand observes that

> Modern Thailand would have been impossible without them [i.e., many of the hard-headed, money-minded Chinese]. The pull into Thai civilization has always been very strong, although little effort was ever exercised by the government. The descendants of Chinese were merely considered to be Thai and treated as such. Citizenship was granted easily. Under an oriental ruling class with whom the Chinese could feel somewhat akin, the process of assimilation continued naturally. This was in contrast to Chinese experience in European-dominated colonies, such as British Malaya or the Philippines, where the Chinese were constantly distinguished as Chinese and where racial prejudice made marriage into the ruling class the exception. Nor was citizenship so readily granted.... Thus the Chinese protectorate system of British Malaya may be cited as an institution which unwittingly prevented Chinese from identifying themselves with the original people of the land and distinguishing them sharply from the ruling class.[9]

The lack of clear-cut ethnic or ideological cleavages and the consequent faction-based fragmentation of elites led one observer to note that "since May 1992, political parties in Thailand have been categorized not along ideological, ethnic, or economic and social policy lines but by a strange criterion of being good or "angelic" parties and bad or "devilish" parties."[10] Yet, the line between being angelic and devilish was not hard and fast, either. This meant that Thai parties were not arrayed along a single dominant cleavage line; there were fundamentally no centrist and no extreme or anti-system parties. Each party was willing to form a postelection coalition with any other party to gain cabinet status. Consequently, the experience of the 1997–8 economic crisis was unlikely to trigger an elite convergence, for, in a unique sense, there was little to converge about.

The Philippines: dominant but tractable ethno-linguistic cleavages

In Chapter 3, I concluded that the Philippine political elite was fragmented, like its Thai counterpart. Yet, the Philippine fragmentation was distinctive in that its primary origin lay in civil society, not in military factions. The Philippine military never dominated the civilian sector. The Marcos government was a civilian regime, even though it was repressive in nature. The Philippines had always been and still is dominated by a collectivity of landed and financial oligarchs, albeit more weakly during Marcos's predatory and sultanistic rule. In other words, fragmented civilian elites were collectively dominant over the military. As a result, the cleavage between civilian and military sectors was not salient in the Philippines.

Nor was the issue of ethnic Chinese salient. Like Thailand, the Philippines does not confront problems arising from an economically dominant but politically weak ethnic Chinese community that might divide the country. "The traditional political elite in the Philippines originated in a primarily Chinese mestizo landowning class that acquired wealth but was denied power under Spanish rule."[11] In fact, Corazon Aquino and Cardinal Sin are Sino-Filipinos. The fact that the ethnic Chinese issue was of limited importance in the Philippines was due, in part, to a distinct US colonial policy that discouraged Chinese immigration.[12]

Except for religious conflicts, the divisive legacies of colonialism, whether Spanish or American, were not especially pronounced. For example, the Spanish Creoles were well assimilated into the native Filipinos.[13] But the southern ethno-religious conflict is a product of both Spanish and American colonialism. American colonial policy encouraged Catholics, the most visible legacy of Spanish rule, to move into historically Muslim areas of Mindanao, which were newly incorporated into the Philippines under US rule.[14] But this ethno-religious conflict, though serious, remained a largely localized issue and was somewhat under control owing to a split within the Muslim movement before the crisis. Finally, US military bases had long been a divisive issue among the elites; however, once the bases were closed in 1992, this issue disappeared.

Indeed, the Philippines displayed a potential for developing nonascriptive or class-based political cleavages. Signs of this were that land reform remained a controversial issue, the Communist Party was continuing activity and appeal even after the end of the Cold War, and antipathy against dominant landowning elites was widespread among the masses. Yet, this cleavage was no more than a potential one at the onset of the economic crisis, and it did not develop into a major political cleavage among the national elite, because leftist elites remained quite weak.

What, then, accounted for the fragmentation of Philippine elites? A study of the 1992 presidential election revealed that an ethno-linguistic cleavage predominated other political cleavages. On the basis of provincial-level aggregate data, Carl Lande found that, "for almost all seven candidates, linguistic regional loyalties played a more important part in determining the sources of their electoral support than did other types of census variables [such as religion, education, income, home ownership, and farm tenancy]."[15] He also observed that, "Among the explanatory census variables in the tables, languages showed most of the strongest correlation coefficients and percentages of variance in votes accounted for after the influence of other variables had been removed."[16]

The fact that ethno-linguistic ties were so important in voters' decisions is not a surprise, given a large number of presidential candidates whose political platforms were not very different from each other and the universal tendency among voters to support their local leaders, other things being more or less equal. Yet, the importance of ethno-linguistic ties between voters and the 1992 presidential candidates requires careful interpretation. First, linguistic diversity in the Philippines was obviously greater than the contending political elite groups displayed in the 1992 election: some 80 languages including eight major ones are the mother tongues of various ethnic groups.[17] This implies that the political parties or national elite groups were probably fragmented for some other reason before they *a posteriori* built up their popular bases by emphasizing their linguistic ties. Second, unlike in Malaysia, ethno-linguistic groups in the Philippines tend not to maintain strong political solidarities *vis-à-vis other ethno-linguistic groups*. Instead, the parochial identities of voters were not socially mobilized in terms of Karl W. Deutsch[18] because local landowning elites, whose fiefdoms barely crossed multiple linguistic groups, remained intact after Marcos's destructive rule. In other words, ties between the political elites and their supporters within particular ethnic groups were apparently based more on nonlinguistic paternalism than on linguistic solidarity or hostility against outsiders. As a result, the ethno-linguistic political cleavage was likely to give way to other cleavages if local patronage networks weakened, although the overall relations *among ethno-linguistic groups* might remain unchanged. In this respect, the ascriptive cleavages in the Philippine politics were much less than intractable.

In short, the existence of a linear political cleavage line cannot be identified in the Philippines. Before the crisis, fragmented elites mobilized political support mostly through ethno-linguistic ties and paternalism. The elites shared similar economic interests. Hence, they did not have much incentive to develop class-based or universalistic political ties to the masses beyond the boundaries of their political fiefdoms; their popular support bases were narrow and localized. Consequently, it would not be easy for Philippine elites to undergo an elite convergence that economic crisis might otherwise trigger.

Convergence attempts and failures

Thailand: Constitutional revision and elite reshuffling

After a series of speculative attacks on the baht during the preceding month, the Thai government finally let it float on July 2, 1997. It was later reported that

"Foreign reserves fell from more than 24 billion dollars to just 2.5 billion dollars in a matter of weeks as the bank [i.e., The Bank of Thailand] tried unsuccessfully to fend off speculative attacks against the currency."[19] The devaluation took place only five days after 16 unsound finance and security companies, including Finance One, had been suspended for 30 days and ordered to arrange mergers. The float also came just two days after Prime Minister Chavalit Yongchaiyudh, in a nationally televised announcement, denied any intention to devaluate the Thai currency. Despite the devaluation, the economy continued to crumble.

On July 17, Finance Minister Thanong Bidaya, who replaced Amnuay Virawan, a defender of a strong baht until his resignation on June 19, visited Thailand's biggest creditor, Japan, to appeal for its help in getting Thailand out of the foreign currency crisis. But Japan did not want to take any action without involvement of the IMF, whose strict conditions made its financial assistance highly unpalatable to Chavalit's coalition government.[20] Meanwhile, the US government downplayed the significance of the currency crisis. Its Treasury officials said, "there appeared to be 'no systemic risk to the international financial system as a whole,'" adding that, "Thailand's present fiscal problems – the result of slowing export growth and the crash of its inflated real estate and banking sectors over the past six months – are nowhere near the magnitude of Mexico's in 1994."[21] The USA did not want to be directly involved in any financial aid package of the kind it engineered during the 1994 Mexican peso crisis, and instead preferred to stand behind a bailout package organized by the IMF.

On August 3, the Thai government agreed with the IMF about a bailout package, even though the details were subject to further discussion. On August 5, the government closed 42 financial and securities companies and increased duties on consumer goods from seven to ten percent. Before these actions, the Bank of Thailand's Financial Institutions Development Fund had pumped in about 1.2 trillion baht (30.8 billion dollars) to keep debt-ridden financial firms afloat.[22]

In this deteriorating situation, the Chavalit government that took power in November 1996 was already in danger of falling; and various calls for Chavalit's resignation were heard. Yet, dissolving the lower house was unpalatable to Chavalit when his popularity plummeted. It was also unbearably expensive for all political parties to go through another election, especially, when they did not fully recoup their electoral expenditures on the 1995 and 1996 general elections as well as when the national economy collapsed.[23] Barring another election, political options were (1) continuation of the coalition government after comprehensive reform, (2) a new government led by the coalition partner Chatichai Choonhavan of the Chart Pattana party, (3) a technocratic government led by an extra-parliamentary figure like Privy Councilor Prem Tinsulanonda that would be backed by the military and King Bhumibol Adulyadej, and (4) the opposition's formation of a government led by Chuan Leekpai of the Democrat Party. This wide range of political options reflected the new democracy's instability, even though a military coup was not seriously considered.

The first option was infeasible because of the coalition government's internal division. In particular, two powerful groups, whose support was indispensable for sustaining the fragile coalition, strongly opposed reform. They were the Chart

Pattana Party, the second largest party in the coalition, and Sanoh Thienthong, the Interior Minister who was a major faction leader and secretary-general of Chavalit's party. Korn Dabbaransi, Industry Minister and heir apparent of Chatichai, denounced the Bank of Thailand's suspension of 42 finance companies in a cabinet meeting. Korn and his Chart Pattana colleague walked out of the meeting after Chavalit defended Chaiyawat Wibulswasdi, the Bank of Thailand governor in his decision.[24] Meanwhile, Interior Minister Sanoh mobilized and brought some 20,000 local leaders to Bangkok on September 5 in an attempt to sabotage a new constitution that, if passed, would erode his department's power.[25]

Only under heavy pressure by military and business leaders did the coalition government agree to accept the new constitution, the major focus of which was cleaning up entrenched political corruption.[26] The key features of the new constitution were as follows:

1   introduction of a mixed election system in which 400 district representatives by plurality rule and 100 representatives by a party list PR system with a single nation-wide constituency are to be elected by voters that cast two separate ballots,
2   popular election of 200 non-partisan senators in province-based multi-member single-vote constituencies by plurality rule,
3   centralized vote-counting,
4   compulsory voting,
5   no senator or parliamentarian holding cabinet ministers,
6   setting-up of an election commission that takes over management of all elections from the Department of Local Administration,
7   and university degree requirements for senators and MPs except former and current parliamentarians and senators.

Final passage of the constitutional draft by 578–16 votes on September 27 allowed Chavalit to win a censure motion against the Prime Minister on the same day and hang on for the moment.[27] As a result, the existing parliament could not be dissolved by the section of 323 of the new constitution for another 240 days, during which three core bills on the election of senators and parliamentarians, on an election commission, and on political parties were required to be finalized and approved.[28]

The second option – a new government by another coalition partner, Chatichai – was not plausible because his party commanded only 52 parliamentary seats out of 393, which would mean greater political fragmentation in the form of a weaker coalition government than the existing six-party coalition. Moreover, Chatichai's party had opposed the reform policies demanded by the IMF, and hence it was unacceptable to international creditors.

The third option – a technocratic government – did not come into being. On October 21, Chavalit called an emergency meeting of cabinet members and security officials amid demonstrations calling for his resignation. At this meeting a state of emergency or a curfew and strict media censorship were rejected by the military, in particular, General Chettha Thanajaro, Army Commander.[29] The military and General Chettha had earlier played the key role in getting the constitution passed, by giving strong support for political reform in the face of elite divisions over the constitution's passage.[30] The king also firmly opposed a nonelected government.[31]

The final option – a new government led by an opposition party – was the most feasible alternative to the existing government. Chuan Leekpai was regarded as relatively clean and honest. He had strong support among Thai business leaders and international creditors, including the IMF, even though he was not as much favored by the urban poor and peasants outside the southern region. In the last general election, Chuan's Democrats had won only 12 of 137 seats in the poorest but most populous northeastern region. This left the Democrats the second largest party next to the New Aspiration Party by two seats. Their greatest strength came from Bangkok and the southern region. Seventy-six of the Democrats' 123 seats were located in Bangkok and the southern region.[32] Nonetheless, as the crisis was largely financial in nature, a Chuan government, supported by the business leaders and international creditors, was best fit to tackle it.

Chavalit successfully formed a new cabinet on October 24, four days after Finance Minister Thanong Bidaya resigned to protest the withdrawal of a three-day-old tax increase on petroleum products. This was Chavalit's last effort to boost public confidence in his leadership. However, his new cabinet failed to regain public confidence; all major coalition party leaders were still in the cabinet, although ten nonpoliticians including finance and commerce ministers were also brought into it.[33] The Thai currency continued to fall. On November 3, Chavalit suddenly announced that he would resign as Prime Minister effective midnight November 6. This was done "on the eve of a special session of parliament called to approve six executive decrees needed to implement urgent financial reforms" and just before the first review of the government's compliance with conditions for the IMF bail-out. Chavalit's announcement occurred on the same day that "military leaders paid him a visit" to make it known that he should resign.[34]

After a few days of tense jockeying for power, Chuan Leekpai emerged as the winner with 208 of 393 parliamentarians on his side, defeating Chatichai of the Chart Pattana Party and becoming Prime Minister of an eight-party coalition government on November 9. Chuan's victory was due to a crucial defection from Chatichai's camp. Against the decision of their party leader, Samak Sundaravej, to stand behind Chatichai, 12 MPs from the outgoing coalition's 18-member strong Prachakorn Thai Party (PTP) joined Chuan's camp and thus gave him an 11-seat majority against the Chatichai camp.[35] The final lineup for the government coalition was Chuan's Democrats (123), Chart Thai (39), Social Action Party (20), Solidarity Party (8), Seritham (4), Palang Dharma and Thai Party (one each), plus the 12 defectors from the PTP.[36] Subsequently, Chuan formed a pro-IMF economic team including Finance Minister Tarrin Nimmanhaeminda. His shaky coalition was strengthened a year later when one of the two major opposition parties, the Chart Pattana Party, joined it.[37]

Thailand thus accomplished a peaceful power transfer without holding a fresh election and without a military coup. However, this required much collusion among the still fragmented elite groups, a collusion leveraged by the IMF. In other words, Thailand had yet to replace elite fragmentation with a consensual configuration pointing toward a more stable regime. It remains an open question whether the new constitutional order will contribute to reducing fragmentation and bringing about a major elite realignment.

The Philippines: Constitutional debate, populism, and communist insurgency

The Asian economic crisis hit the Philippines when it had just extricated itself from a seemingly endless economic recession and it was poised to exit from the IMF's Extended Fund Facility.[38] The crisis also coincided with the end of Fidel V. Ramos's six-year presidential term. At the start of September 1997, before the regional crisis had fully developed, Ramos and close advisors, such as Executive Secretary Ruben Torres and Budget Secretary Salvador Enriquez, tried to extend his term by revising the constitution's six-year term limit. They believed that the Ramos administration's economic performance had been excellent, and that Ramos was the right person to fend off a full-blown crisis. They did not trust the popular prospective presidential candidate, Vice President Joseph Ejercito Estrada, to do this. Their concern was that populist Estrada would dismantle Ramos's economic achievements that were based on economic liberalism and market opening. Given Estrada's popularity, they thought that none other than Ramos could prevail against Estrada. In other words, they did not want to risk losing power to their political opponent by following the existing constitutional rules. To deal with the looming crisis, they wanted to deviate from the game rules.

Some congressmen and senators including General Jose Almonte, the president's national security advisor, jumped on this bandwagon. Eight senators and 87 members of Congress were also barred from seeking reelection under constitutional term limits because the 1987 constitution put two-term and three-term limits on senators and members of Congress, respectively.[39] House Concurrent Resolution 40 was introduced for the purpose of changing the constitution in this respect, calling for Congress to convene as a constituent assembly to study and propose relevant amendments.

The constitutional change movement, popularly known as "chacha," formed a popular movement, People's Initiative for Reform, Modernization, and Action (PRIMA) and launched a signature collection campaign.[40] The PRIMA, which means signature in Filipino, claimed to collect more than six million signatures to approve the proposed amendments.

Watching this constitutional move by Ramos, the business elite at first responded by saying that it would be acceptable only if the term extension move did nothing to worsen the economic situation.[41] Later, however, business leaders openly opposed the change when the economy further deteriorated. Given that the Asian economic crisis had not yet reached its full extent, some business leaders thought that the Philippine economic deterioration was primarily attributable to Ramos's term limit extension moves.

The harshest opposition to the chacha came from the Catholic Church and its head, Manila Cardinal Sin. Cardinal Sin had been opposed to the Ramos administration over the issue of family planning (aside from the fact that Ramos was a Protestant). Although a vehement opponent of Vice President Estrada's presidential candidacy, Sin's first priority was to get Ramos's term renewal blocked. Sin was uncertain whether Estrada would in fact win an election, and he wanted to be kingmaker in the anti-Estrada camp. Another prominent opponent of Ramos's term extension was none other than former President Aquino who had supported Ramos's election in 1992. She worried that a term extension would lead to a return of a Marcos-like authoritarian rule, and her own 1987 constitution was precisely intended to prevent any possibility of this.

Leftists, including Chito Gascon, human rights activist and executive director of the National Institute for Policy Studies, formed the Samba (the Saligang Adhikain ng Mamamayan-Bantayan or Defend the People's Basic Aspiration) to protest against the chacha. Extreme leftists formed another movement, the Lambada (Labanan ng Mamamayan ang Bagong Diktadurya or Citizens' Fight against a New Dictatorship) against the chacha.[42]

Because the national elites were so divided over the prolonged constitutional change and could not reach any agreement, they resorted to mass rallies to demonstrate their respective popular strengths. Anti-chacha elites staged a mass rally in Manila on September 21, which was the 25th anniversary of the declaration of martial law by Ferdinand Marcos. The pro-chacha elites held their own mass rally, with Ramos present, in Davao City in Mindanao the day before. At that rally, Ramos said, "I will not run for re-election. Period. Period. Period." Still, suspecting his intentions, about 50,000 people flocked to the anti-chacha rally in Manila, led by Cardinal Sin, former President Aquino, and many prominent business people.[43] After both rallies, Ramos backed off and held private meetings with Cardinal Sin and Aquino. Subsequently, the constitutional amendment issue seemed to subside.[44]

The heated debates about constitutional change indicated that some elites still held ambivalent commitments to the basic rules of the game. The elites resorted to mass rallies to resolve their constitutional disagreement, rather than going through formal channels or making a deal with opponent elites, and this skirmish suggested a continuing lack of elite consensus or mutual trust. They did not seriously discuss the issue of constitutional change with regard to the utility of Ramos's economic policies in a crisis situation. Instead, their arguments were full of the populist rhetoric. This was why the anti- and pro-chacha camps quickly disintegrated once the status quo was reaffirmed and the presidential election contest took center stage.

In the May 1998 presidential election, which was concurrently held with other congressional and local elections, 11 candidates stood initially.[45] However, one of them, Imelda Marcos, dropped out and endorsed the leading candidate, Vice President Estrada. The final official election results are presented in Table 5.1.[46]

Despite the large number of presidential candidates, the effective number was 4.35. This was significantly smaller than the 5.77 effective candidates in 1992. In

Table 5.1 Results of the 1998 Philippine presidential election (per cent)

Joseph Ejercito Estrada	39.86
Joe C. de Venecia, Jr	15.87
Raul Roco	13.83
Emilio Mario R. Osmena	12.44
Alfredo S. Lim	8.71
Renato de Villa	4.86
Miriam Santiago	2.96
Juan Ponce Enrile	1.28
Santiago Dumlao	0.12
Manuel Morato	0.07
Total	100

1998, Estrada secured 39.86 percent of the national vote, whereas the winner in 1992, Ramos, had obtained only 24 percent. This wide lead by Estrada and the consequent decrease in the effective number of presidential candidates would favor elite convergence.

Estrada's outright victory was largely due to two factors. One was that three opposition political parties united to field a single presidential candidate, Estrada, whereas the ruling party was divided among three candidates. The other factor was the successful image making of Estrada as champion of the poor. At first, four opposition parties agreed to merge and field a united presidential candidate. They were Estrada's Partido ng Masang Pilipino Party (PMP), Senator Edgardo Angara's Laban ng Demokratikong Pilipino (Laban), Ernesto Maceda and Eduardo Cojuangco's National People's Coalition (NPC), and Miriam Santiago's People's Reform Party (PRP).[47] Later, Santiago stayed out of the agreement, and the three parties formed a new opposition party, Laban ng Makabayang Masang Pillipino (LMMP), with Laban Chairperson Angara and NPC President Maceda as its president and chair-person, respectively.[48]

On the other hand, the governing party, Lakas ng Edsa-National Union of Christian Democrats-United Muslim Democratic Party (Lakas or Lakas-NUCD), was divided over the nomination of its presidential candidate. In the end, Lakas nominated Jose de Venecia as its official candidate, and Ramos also endorsed him. Yet, two other candidates also entered the race. They were Renato de Villa and Emilio Osmena. De Villa, who was former Defense Secretary and had been known as Ramos's colon, ran as independent spoiler candidate after being passed over by the president. Osmena, who was chief economic advisor to President Ramos and his 1992 running mate, wanted to reorient the focus of economic development from the central area to provinces, capitalizing on his economic success story in Cebu. He formed the party of Probinsya Muna Development Initiatives (Back to the Provinces Development Initiatives, or Promdi).

Even though crime and corruption, women's rights, and rural development were campaign issues, highlighted by Lim, Roco, and Osmena,[49] respectively, the most salient issue was economic inequality among the classes. De Venecia

Table 5.2 Philippine presidential candidates' vote percentages among the top six linguistic groups

	I	II	III	IV*	V	VI	VII	VIII	IX	X	N
Tagalog	0.06	0.01	0.00	0.55	0.17	0.01	0.00	0.00	0.19	0.02	2.75
Cebuano	0.10	0.02	0.00	0.60	0.04	0.01	0.00	0.19	0.03	0.00	2.42
Ilonggo	0.06	0.01	0.00	0.55	0.12	0.00	0.00	0.07	0.05	0.13	2.85
Ilocano	0.37	0.03	0.03	0.45	0.00	0.00	0.00	0.00	0.12	0.00	2.83
Kapampangan	0.11	0.00	0.02	0.65	0.10	0.00	0.02	0.00	0.10	0.00	2.19
Bicol	0.00	0.00	0.00	0.14	0.00	0.00	0.00	0.00	0.86	0.00	1.32

Source: Social Weather Stations Post-election Survey, SWR98-II.
Note: The columns show ten presidential candidates, de Venecia, de Villa, Enrile, Estrada, Lim, Marcos, Morato, Osmena, Roco, Santiago in order from left to right, and the last column shows the effective number of presidential candidates for each language group. None of the respondents answered that they had voted for Dumlao, and some still answered that they had voted for Imelda Marcos, even though she dropped out.

advocated the continuation of Ramos's neoliberal economic policies that favored middle classes while Estrada championed the poor. This conflict between rich and poor was the major deriving force behind Estrada's wide lead and the decrease in the effective number of candidates. Echoing the ordinary poor's view, said a villager in the main southern island of Mindanao, "I will vote for Estrada because they say he is for the poor." "I have not seen him personally, but I will vote for him just the same. He seems sincere and approachable unlike the others who will listen only to the rich when elected."[50] Estrada's poor supporters were unabashed by his past activities of womanizing, gambling, and heavy drinking. Their unabated support for Estrada was characterized as "a revenge of the masses" by an opposition legislator.[51] The poverty incidence[52] in 1997 was 32.1 percent, and it must have been much higher right before the May election, taking into account −0.5 percent GDP growth in 1998.[53]

The hypothesis that the poorer the more inclined voters were to support Estrada was confirmed by a Social Weather Stations survey. All survey respondents were grouped into three socioeconomic classes: the upper (8%), middle (71%), and lower (21%). The survey seems to have over-represented the middle class: their size was too large given the absolute poverty rate of over 32 percent. Yet, it showed an overall trend. Of the lower class, 47.7 percent voted for Estrada, whereas 37.9 percent of the middle class and 23.9 percent of the upper class did.[54] None of the classes overwhelmingly supported Estrada. Even a majority of the lower class did not vote for him. Nonetheless, the lower class was more inclined to support him than any other class.

The same survey data also showed that the poor were more homogeneous in their voting choices. Consequently, they greatly contributed to reducing the effective number of candidates: the effective number of candidates was 5.17 within the upper class, 4.62 within the middle class, and 3.49 within the lower class. In other words, the upper class was more divided than any other socioeconomic class. This suggests that the fragmentation in the Philippines originated in the upper strata.

This rise of class cleavage meant that the previously most important voting cleavage, ethno-linguistic ties, had comparatively declined. Estrada won the largest vote in 16 of the 23 linguistic groups included in the above-mentioned survey. As seen in Table 5.2, he was the plurality or majority winner in all the six largest linguistic groups except Bicolanos, which together accounted for 87 percent of the total respondents: Tagalog, Ilocano, Ilonggo, Cebuano, Bicolano, and Kapampangan. Estrada's support rates ranged from 45 percent to 65 percent, aside from the Bicolanos that overwhelmingly preferred their native candidate, Roco. In short, regardless of languages at home, most voters supported Estrada.

However, we cannot conclude that such ethno-linguistic ties did not matter at all in 1998. Rather, they still mattered; their salience just declined. Some linguistic groups including Bicolanos still solidly voted for their homeland candidates. At the same time, candidates other than two or three were virtually invisible in every language group. This meant that candidates other than two or three were in a great disadvantage in every language group. The last column of the table shows, first, that the effective number of candidates for any linguistic group was far smaller than the national average, 4.35. Second, the variation in the effective number of candidates was not as wide among linguistic groups as among socioeconomic classes, excluding the Bicolanos. The modal variation in the effective number of candidates among linguistic groups was only 0.66 points; by contrast, the corresponding value for socioeconomic classes was 2.21 points. These two facts prove that the candidate choices of linguistic groups were quite selective or narrow-ranged. Note that even though each linguistic group preferred only two or three candidates, the effective number of candidates at the national level was still high. This is because each linguistic group had a different combination of two or three most-preferred candidates, even though Estrada was the most popular in almost all linguistic groups. In sum, ethno-linguistic ties were no longer the most salient, but they still affected the viability of presidential candidates.

Despite the rise of class cleavage and the consequent decline of ethno-linguistic ties, which would favor elite convergence, there were negative factors. First, Estrada's overwhelming victory came from his personal populist appeals and hence, was hardly so sustainable and repeatable as to force his political opponents to unite against him and form another power bloc in the future. His coalition partners were not considered champions of the poor or leftists or center-leftists. For instance, Eduardo Cojuangco was a well-known former Marcos business confidant. In addition, Estrada won the election only after he spent the largest amount of money among all candidates, 111.4 million pesos. Moreover, of the total expenditure, only 2 million, 1.8 percent, came from his pockets. Notable contributors were Banker Edgardo Espiritu, his Finance Secretary (P3 million), business person Jose Pardo, his Secretary of Trade and Industry (P1 million), and Eduardo Cojuangco's brother, Henry Cojuangco (P2.5 million).[55] In short, the regrouping of such elite groups around Estrada was not a sustainable alliance of pro-poor groups. More likely, it was a temporary populist coalition that took advantage of his personal popularity among the masses. The masses, in turn, just wanted a back-lash against traditionally powerful oligarchic groups; they did not have strong preference for Estrada himself.

Furthermore, ironically, the economic crisis that helped Estrada to become president left him no financial resources. This made him difficult to live up to his campaign slogan, "Erap for the Poor." "I was frustrated in my first few weeks as president," Estrada noted,

> I found out the so-called emerging tiger that was the Philippines was just a kitten. The vaunted economic growth was not there. And the government had no money. I promised so much to the poor and I found out I didn't have the money to carry out those promises.[56]

As a result, it was doubtful that populist Estrada would implement successful pro-poor policies against its coalition partners' strong business interests and with virtually empty government coffers.

Second, traditional oligarchs, who were responsible for Philippine fragmentation, still maintained their political power. Take the clan of the Aquino/Cojuangcos for example.

> Aquino's 33-year-old son, Benigno 'Noynoy' Aquino III, is running for Congress in the second district of their home province of Tarlac north of Manila. His slogan is: 'Ninoy Yesterday, Noynoy Today.' Cory's sister-in-law, Tesssie Aquino Oreta, wife of the mayor of a suburban Manila town, is running for senator. (Tessie's brother has himself been senator since People Power and is now trying for Congress.) Cory's own brother, Congressman Jose 'Peping' Cojuangco Jr., cannot contest again, having already served the maximum number of three terms in Tarlac's first district. He is instead backing someone unrelated. If Peping's protege loses, it will likely to be a nephew – so Peping wins either way. His wife is running for her third term as Tarlac's governor. An uncle of Ninoy's, Herminio Aquino, he is her vice-gubernatorial running mate. A longtime Peping political ally is opposing his wife, so, again, he cannot lose. An Aquino relation is seeking the third congressional district seat given up by Herminio after he hit the three-term limit.[57]

In addition, Emilio Osmena was the patriarch of the dominant clan in central Cebu province, and his cousin was the running mate of Lim, Liberal Party presidential candidate. Vice President-elect Gloria Macapagal Arroyo belonged to the clan of the Macapagals, based in Pampanga, the second largest province of Central Luzon. Raul Roco belonged to a dominant landed family in Bicol, an eastern province.[58]

The last obstacle to elite convergence is institutional. First, there are three different representatives who equally claim the nationwide mandate: president, vice president, and 24 senators. Of the 12 senators whose terms of office are not coterminous with the outgoing president or vice president, anyone ambitious feels free to bid for presidency without any risk of losing his or her current senatorial status.

> In the May 11 elections, three senators with unfinished terms ran for President: Raul Roco, Miriam Defensor Santiago and Juan Ponce Enrile. Three other senators ran for Vice President: Francisco Tatad, Sergio Osmena III and Gloria Macapagal Arroyo. Gloria Arroyo won as Vice President .... The five others who lost in the elections will continue to finish their 6-year terms which end in the year 2001.[59]

Second, the single-term limit for presidents is another institutional feature that encourages political fragmentation.[60] It shortens the time horizon of key players and makes it difficult for an incumbent president to keep the solidarity of his political party or coalition. Given this, it is not odd for Ramos's governing party to split up right before the presidential election, even in the face of formidable Estrada. In addition, both the first and second presidents after the 1986 democratization made futile attempts to extend their terms by getting rid of the constitutional term limit. These moves, which divided up the national elites and were frustrated only by mass rallies, undermined the nascent democratic institution.

In sum, we indeed observed the overwhelming victory by a populist candidate, the rise of class cleavage, and the decrease in the effective presidential candidates after the economic crisis. Nonetheless, this apparent elite realignment, which was largely due to Estrada's personal populist image, is not durable. I now move to the issue of whether the economic crisis contributed to taming the anti-system party, the Communist Party of the Philippines.[61]

A good indicator of the communists' moderation will be a comprehensive formal peace agreement with the government. Peace negotiations between the government and the communists that started in June 1995 had been recessed without reaching any agreements on substantive issues after the fourth round of formal talks in April 1997. The first formal negotiations after the outbreak of the economic crisis started in the Netherlands on January 5, 1998 and ended on January 11. The government peace panel was led by former ambassador Howard Dee, and the communist counterpart was headed by NDFP (National Democratic Front of the Philippines) executive committee member Luis Jalandoni.[62] After another round of talks, they finally signed the Comprehensive Agreement on Human Rights and International Humanitarian Law on March 16.[63] Under this agreement, "the government shall 'work for the immediate repeal of any subsisting repressive laws, decrees or other executive issuances.'" Both sides "agreed to 'respect and support rights' of the victims of human rights violations during the Martial Law, particularly the 10,000 victims claiming damages from the estate of the late President Ferdinand Marcos."[64] With this agreement, they closed one of the four substantive issues on the agenda of peace negotiations. The other three issues were social and economic reforms, political and constitutional reforms, and cessation of hostilities and disposition of armed forces.

The negotiation teams also exchanged drafts of the proposed pact on social and economic reforms. The Ramos government wanted to reach an accord on two more components of the peace agreement, social and economic reforms and political and constitutional reforms, but it did not succeed. As a result, the other components of the peace pact had to be negotiated with Estrada's new government.[65]

The Estrada government did not show as strong political will as the predecessor to pursue peace talks with the communists.[66] Estrada started his term with a warning, "Huwag ninyo akong subukan (Don't test me)." In July 1998, Jose Ma Sison, the founder of the Communist Party of the Philippines, claimed, "the current economic turmoil provides an opportunity to reverse the movement's decline since the early 1990s." He also claimed that the Estrada regime was against the poor and controlled by big businesses and landlords. "He specifically criticized the plan of the Estrada administration to continue free market policies of the Ramos administration, including liberalization, privatization and deregulation."[67]

On February 24, 1999, lukewarm peace talks with the communists came to a complete breakdown. Estrada unilaterally and indefinitely suspended peace talks with the NDFP a week after communist rebels kidnapped Brigadier General Victor Obillo and his aide and two days after Central Police District Chief Inspector Roberto Bernal was also abducted.[68] The general was a classmate of Armed Forces Chief General Joselin Nazareno at the Philippine Military Academy and the highest-ranking officer that had ever been taken hostage by communist insurgents.

After communist insurgents released all their captives without obtaining any concessions from the government in April, another round of formal talks seemed set to start. However, Estrada earlier set two more conditions for resuming talks, which were unacceptable to the NDFP: talks should be held within the country and should be finished by December.[69] CPP founding chairperson Sison made a counterproposal, saying that peace talks might be held in the country, but only if they were held in one of the alleged 81 NPA guerrilla fronts nationwide.[70] Besides these issues, they disagreed on which legal framework to use in implementing the previous human rights agreement.

> The government says it cannot but uphold the Constitution as its only guideline in this pact's implementation, while the NDFP says observing the same guideline would be tantamount to 'capitulation.' Instead, the rebels want their bylaws and international agreements on human rights as guidelines.[71]

While formal talks between the government and the communists led to nowhere over these obstacles and the Senate's ratification of the Visiting Forces Agreement,[72] some communists surrendered to the government. For instance, in April 1999, 204 rebels including two NPA commanders surrendered. The government set aside 252 hectares of land for those returnees and promised to provide funds for a livestock project to help them to settle down.[73]

Yet, other reports showed the contrary postcrisis trend that the communists strengthened their ranks, which had been steadily on the decline over the last few years. In February 1999, Presidential Spokesperson Fernando Barican confirmed reports that NPA guerrillas in the the Agusan del Sur, Surigao del Sur and Compostela Valley areas "increased by 351 to 2,341 guerrillas between 1997 and 1998. The number of firearms held by the armed wing of the Communist Party of the Philippines also reportedly increased by 259."[74]

In sum, after the economic crisis, the Ramos government successfully concluded the first component of the proposed peace agreements with the communists. However, three more components were yet to be concluded before the communists were fully integrated into normal politics. Unlike Ramos, however, populist Estrada took a hard-line stance in dealing with communist insurgents. He rejected Cardinal Sin's and El Shaddai leader Mike Velarde's offers to broker the resumption of peace talks. As overconfident Estrada did not actively pursue peace agreements with the communists, an early complete peace pact with communists would be unlikely. In an interview with *the Far Eastern Economic Review* on June 17, 1999, Estrada said, "If we don't show our strength now, it will be the next generations who will be suffering. I've told them: if you don't like peace talks, let's go to war. I'm determined if necessary to wipe them out."[75] Meanwhile, the effects of the economic crisis on communist activities were mixed. The communists' unconditional release of all captives demonstrated that they now lost much of their previous bargaining power with the government. Yet, the weakening communists were somewhat successful in recruiting after the economic crisis, even thought they did no longer pose a *serious* threat to the new democratic regime.

Conclusion

Thailand, which had no clear identified political cleavage, simply reshuffled the same elite stock without going to the public and formed a new cabinet that would tackle the economic crisis. There was no elite circulation. Nor was there any meaningful realignment that would last long. The military played a prominent role in this reshuffling by refusing a coup. Yet, during the crisis, which made the masses charged intensely, the Thai elites succumbed to the popular demand for constitutional reform. The new constitution was mainly designed to clean up corrupted politicians. We have yet to see how much the new rules of the game will help to get the old stock political elite out and bring in a new stock and cut down the excessive number of political parties. Yet, an elite convergence will be unlikely without creating durable political cleavages. One such possibility in Thailand would be an urban versus rural cleavage.

The Philippines, which had a dominant yet tractable linguistic cleavage, witnessed the rise of populism during the constitutional debates at the early stage of the economic crisis and in the 1998 presidential election. The populism attempted to mobilize the unidentified people in general during the constitutional debates and the poor in particular in the 1998 presidential election. Interestingly, as a result of the mobilization of the poor, the major political cleavage shifted from ethno-linguistic ties to classes. This in turn helped to reduce its excessive number of meaningful political elite groups in the 1998 presidential election. However, Estrada's populist electoral coalition was unsustainable, and it did not appear to induce the remaining elite groups to form a solid counter-group. This was because his populism was primarily based on his personal image and lacked any organizational base. Finally, his populist government did not go well with the Communist Party, even though both claimed to represent the same constituency, the poor. Rather, Estrada, who was overconfident of his popularity among the poor, took a hostile position toward the anti-regime party. Consequently the Philippine elite did not undergo the process of elite convergence in the face of the economic crisis. I believe that this is due, primarily, to the fact that the Philippine elite had not been fragmented along a linear cleavage line at the onset of the economic crisis. The Philippines's relatively mild experience of the economic crisis may be another possible explanation for the nonoccurrence of elite convergence. Yet, however serious the economic crisis in the Philippines had been, the elite still would have resorted to populism, given its precrisis elite cleavages.

6 Economic crisis, consensual elites, and prospects for the further consensus

Chapters 4 and 5 discussed whether nonconsensual elites could become consensual amid an economic crisis. This chapter deals with change in the already quite consensual elite configurations of Malaysia and South Korea, even though our cases are not fully consensual. It first deals with the semiconsensual elite in Malaysia, where a supermajority elite group (National Front) ruled before the crisis. Malaysia's elite consensus was engendered as a legacy of British colonialism, later strengthened and maintained through living historical memory and continuing fear of ethnic conflict, following the 1969 communal riots, and had not since been seriously challenged until the Asian economic crisis occurred.

My main interest with regard to Malaysia is whether its elite differentiation increased as a result of the Asian economic crisis. In particular, I am interested in whether the crisis resulted in a breakup of the supermajority elite group and in the extent to which the rigid ethnic voting became more fluid. The demise or decline of a supermajority elite group, especially in a semi-democracy like Malaysia, requires not only its internal breakup but also the existence of a certain number of cross-voters.[1]

In passing, note that an extremely large magnitude of cross-voting or a great swing of voters from one election to another could also destabilize a political system by making a party system unstable and making it impossible to implement coherent public policies. Thus, only a moderate range of cross-voting is likely to be conducive to democratic stability; cross-voting should be great enough to change governments but not so great as to destabilize a party system.

Quite apart from the effects of the Asian economic crisis, the ethnic alliance in Malaysia will inevitably change because the proportion of the ethnic Chinese population is steadily decreasing and Malay control of the economy has increased as a result of the New Economic Policy and its successor, the New Development Policy.

> The ethnic composition of Malaysia will continue to change markedly in the period of 2021 as a result of differentials in ethnic growth rates. Among Malaysian citizens, Bumiputera growth rates will be more than double those of the Chinese and almost double those of the Indians. Thus, the Bumiputera group is projected to steadily increase its share of Malaysia's total population from 61 percent in 1991 to 70 percent in 2021.[2]

In addition, driven by state policies that favor Malay firms, Malay ownership of capital has significantly increased, though it still accounts for a much smaller portion compared with that of the Chinese or of foreigners. For instance, in 1970, the Bumiputera owned 2.4 percent of the share capital in limited companies; the Chinese owned 27.2 percent, and foreigners owned 63.4 percent. Yet, by 1995 the Bumiputera ownership had increased to 20.6 percent, the Chinese owned 40.9 percent, and foreign ownership had dropped to 27.7 percent.[3] These socioeconomic and demographic changes will ultimately lead to a break-up or major transformation of the National Front alliance by fueling intra-Malay elite conflict and by weakening ties between Malay and Chinese elites. The issue in this chapter is whether the Asian economic crisis helped to speed up this long-term trend by creating extensive cross-voting and intra-Malay elite conflicts.

In South Korea, meanwhile, as noted in Chapter 3, a comprehensive elite consensus about the political noninvolvement of the military gradually emerged, so that there was no military threat to the new democratic regime by the time of the currency crisis. Despite their agreement about the military's political neutrality, South Korean elites had yet to build up a solid consensus on many socioeconomic issues, however. The political alignments did not reflect socioeconomic cleavages but rather, policy-neutral regional cleavages. As no socioeconomic issues were seriously contested in elections, there was no opportunity to ascertain majority views on contentious socioeconomic issues. This meant that elected governments did not have a clear mandate to pursue specific policies. They were instead given virtual carte blanche about the policy line to pursue. Consequently, South Korea often displayed both a tendency toward delegative democracy, including a feeble rule of law, and wide swings in socioeconomic policies. In addition to the rigidity of regional cleavages, the concentration of national assets in a few industrial oligarchs kept elite differentiation somewhat limited, although South Korean democracy was significantly pluralist.

Given these precrisis conditions in South Korea, the key issue is whether the economic crisis helped the elite to build consensus on socioeconomic issues and become more differentiated. This process entails a shift in the rigid regional cleavage structure, which was the root cause of many distortions in Korean democracy after 1987. The process also includes a substantial transformation of the chaebols, which not only enhances the differentiation and competition of economic elites but also makes the political sphere more differentiated by diversifying sources of financial support for political elites. Under this scenario, however, greater elite consensus requires more than just sound macroeconomic performance after the crisis passed.

Malaysia

Post-crisis economic policies and elite realignments before the 1999 general election

In an attempt to forestall the economic crisis, Malaysia initially adopted an austerity economic package consisting of IMF-style policies. This policy package was coordinated by Deputy Prime Minister and Finance Minister Anwar Ibrahim. Included in the package were curbs on credit growth, increased interest rates, redefinition of non-performing loans (NPLs), and cuts in government expenditure.[4]

However, such policies that focused on domestic economic factors had little effect in controlling the currency crisis, once the regional crisis worsened. Consequently, in January 1998, Prime Minister Mahathir, who strongly suspected that the crisis was a collusion of rapacious international financiers, established a separate economic policy coordination body, the National Economic Action Committee (NEAC), whose executive director was Daim Zainuddin, Mahathir's trusted assistant, UMNO (United Malay National Organization) treasurer and former finance minister.

Accordingly, the standard deflationary measures were diluted and then reversed, so that the policy focus shifted noticeably from austerity to boosting economic growth in mid-1998. First, in February 1998, the Statutory Reserve Requirement (SRR) was reduced from 13.5 percent to 10 percent. After three more cuts, it fell to four percent by September 1998. In June, Pengurusan Danaharta Nasional Berhad was established to dispose the NPLs of banking institutions. Danamodal Nasional Berhad was set up to inject capital and increase the capital adequacy ratio of banking institutions. Daim also entered the cabinet as Special Functions Minister, with ambiguous duties. Along with the set-up of the NEAC, Daim's appointment was intended to check the influence of Finance Minister Anwar, who was until then Mahathir's heir apparent. On August 3, the central bank's intervention rate was reduced from 11 percent to 10.5 percent. The rate further went down to 10 percent within a week, and then to 9.5 percent by August 27. On August 28, it was announced that the governor and deputy governor of the central bank had resigned over economic policy disputes. In a statement, Deputy Finance Minister Affifudin Omar said that both men were "professionals who insist on following theories 100 percent" and "ha[d] different views and methods from the government in handling the economic downturn and ha[d] disagreed with the government in its decision to lower the interest rates."[5] Finance Minister Anwar, along with the central bank, favored IMF-style policies, in particular, a tight monetary regime.

This economic policy reversal culminated with the dramatic imposition of capital controls on September 1, which was a measure that the NEAC began to discuss as early as the preceding January. Bank Negara acting governor Zeti Akhtar Aziz announced, among other measures, that the ringgit would be valueless outside Malaysia effective October 1. This measure was intended to repatriate an estimated 25 to 32 billion offshore ringgit, located mostly in Singapore. This amount of offshore ringgit was greater than the approximately 20 billion ringgit inside Malaysia.[6] In addition, foreign portfolio investment could not be withdrawn from Malaysia for a year after coming in, a measure aimed at stopping the destabilizing speculative capital flows.[7] On the next day, the exchange rate of the ringgit to the US dollar was fixed at 3.8.

On September 2, one day after taking these daring market-stabilizing measures, Anwar, who was not wholly in favor of the policy shift, was finally removed from his positions as Deputy Prime Minister and Finance Minister without clear explanation. The next day, to everyone's astonishment, the police filed affidavits that charged Anwar with sodomy and abuses of power to cover up his alleged sexual affairs, as well as posing a threat to national security.[8] Subsequently, Anwar was unanimously expelled from UMNO at a Supreme Council meeting that extended beyond the midnight on September 3. Accordingly, he lost his positions of UMNO Deputy President and Penang UMNO Chief. Anwar's dismissal via criminal allegations was a dramatic move by Mahathir. It not only helped Mahathir to shift public attention from economic policy disputes to a personal issue of sexuality, but also kept his principal opponent preoccupied with mounting legal defense against the allegations of homosexual activities, something that is taboo in the Malay Islamic culture. Thereafter, Anwar was engaged in trading salvos of confusing and exhausting allegations about his sexual activities with Mahathir's camp.

Anwar's dismissal and expulsion were followed by his appearances at public rallies or "road-shows" from September 11 until he was arrested on September 20 under the Internal Security Act. Subsequently, he made a shocking appearance in court on September 29 with a black eye, claiming that he was beaten by the police.

A week after Anwar's arrest, the three opposition parties – Parti Islam Se Malaysia (PAS), Parti Rakyat Malaysia (PRM or Malaysian People's Party), and Democratic Action Party (DAP) – formed Majlis Gerakan Keadilan Rakyat Malaysia (Gerak or Malaysian People's Justice Movement). They also enlisted nongovernment organizations, including Angkatan Belia Islam Malaysia (ABIM or Malaysian Muslim Youth Organization), an organization founded by Anwar in 1974.[9]

Seven months after Anwar's sacking, in April 1999, his followers established Parti Keadilan Nasional (Keadilan or National Justice Party), with Anwar's wife Wan Azizah Wan Ismail as President and former Universiti Malaya lecturer and social activist Chandra Muzaffar as Deputy President. The three vice presidents were former Penang mufti Sheikh Azmi Ahmad, former UMNO Supreme Council member Marina Yusoff, and NGO activist Chua Tian Chang. A former ABIM president was the party's secretary general, and Anwar's former political secretary was appointed its Youth Movement's head. Notably, however, Anwar himself was not a member of the party.[10] A draft of its election manifesto, Agenda for Change, unveiled in July 1999, sought, among other aims, to introduce a two-term limit for Prime Ministers, to repeal the Internal Security Act, and to require all members of parliament and state assemblies to declare their and their families' assets.[11] In short, Anwar and his chief allies adopted what amounted to a full-blown democratization program.[12]

Whether the "mosquito party"[13] formed by Anwar's supporters would fundamentally destabilize UMNO and the ruling coalition, the National Front (BN), depended ultimately on how well it would cooperate with the other established opposition parties in the coming election. The splinter party succeeded in forming Barisan Alternatif (Alternative Front or BA) with three other old opposition parties, PAS, DAP, and PRM.[14] In June 1999, the opposition front agreed to draw up a common manifesto and to field only one candidate to face BN in each electoral district.[15] The opposition formed two technical committees to craft the manifesto and to decide on candidates in the election. PAS spiritual leader Nik Abdul Aziz Nik Mat, who was also Chief of the Council of Islamic Theologians and Kelantan Menteri Besar, said that PAS would drop its insistence on an immediate Islamic state to show its cooperation with other political parties, even though it would retain its commitment to Islam and an Islamic state.[16]

In the next month, the opposition front agreed to uphold the basic principles of the Malaysian constitution that were believed to guarantee political stability and racial harmony. These were constitutional monarchy, parliamentary democracy, human rights, rule of law, judiciary independence, citizenship rights and responsibilities, Islam as the official religion but also the principle of freedom of worship, Bahasa Melayu as the national and official language but also the freedom to use and learn other languages, and a federal system of government. Subsequently, they discussed using a common symbol and name and creating a collective leadership, in addition to the crafting of a common manifesto and allocation of candidates.

In September 1999, the opposition front proposed Anwar as its candidate for Prime Minister. However, understanding that he could not assume the position because of his six-year jail sentence,[17] it added that it would endorse anyone from its ranks that commanded a majority support in the parliament. In the following month, the opposition parties unveiled their joint manifesto representing their consensus and omitting disagreements such as PAS's proposal for an Islamic state. Unlike the governing National Front coalition, they, however, agreed not to use a common symbol, respecting each other's ideological commitments. Their joint manifesto included, among other items, income tax cuts, poverty eradication, assistance of small and medium size businesses as well as introduction of a two-term limit to the positions of Prime Minister, Menteri Besar (Chief Minister in states without Sultans), and Chief Minister.

Against this backdrop, Mahathir finally dissolved the parliament effective November 11, after the widely expected calling of a general election amid economic recovery was delayed due to the eruption of a scandal about Anwar's alleged arsenic poisoning in September 1999.[18] Days earlier, the government announced an expansionary budget for 2000. Its primary feature was that 880,000 civil servants would receive, among other benefits, a one-month bonus along with a one-percent personal income tax cut and a 10 percent basic salary increase.[19]

Post-crisis elite realignments toward greater elite consensus

In the nine-day campaign preceding the November 29 general election, there was a straight fight between BN (National Front) and BA (Alternative Front) in most of the electoral districts. The election results are given in Table 6.1. The most significant difference between the 1995 and 1999 elections was that UMNO lost 17 seats. As a result, even though BN retained a supermajority (148 of 193 seats), UMNO's parliamentary seats were reduced to less than half of the total BN seats.

Table 6.1 1999 Malaysian parliamentary election results

	1995		1999	
	Seats (n)	*Votes (%)*	*Seats (n)*	*Votes (%)*
BN	162	64.96%	148	56.45%
(UMNO)	(89)	n.a.	(72)	n.a.
DAP (BA)	9	12.03	10	12.75
PAS (BA)	7	7.57	27	14.98
Keadilan (BA)	n.a.	n.a	5	11.55
PRM (BA)	0	.66	0	1.03
Semangat 46	6	10.17	n.a	n.a
PBS	8	3.30	3	2.16
Others	0	1.32	0	1.08
Opposition Totals	30	35.04	45	43.55
Totals	192	100	193	100
Turnout		71.86		71.7
Uncontested seats		11		1

Source: "Results" in *New Straits Times*, 1 December 1999; *Bernama* at http://bernama.spr.gov.my; and Research and Information Services, *Elections in Malaysia: A Handbook of Facts and Figures on The Elections: 1955–1995* (Kuala Lumpur: The New Straits Times Press, 1999).

This happened for the first time since the August 1974 general election, which was held one month after the birth of BN.[20] UMNO, on its own, had 25 seats less than a simple majority in parliament, compared with eight seats less than a majority after the 1995 election. This outcome meant that UMNO would have to rely more on the smaller BN component parties for any constitutional revision or simple-majority legislation in parliament. The previously almost unchecked power of UMNO in BN would be more limited because of this electoral shift.

The decline of Malay-dominant UMNO in the government camp was contrasted to the remarkable advance of another Malay party, PAS, in the opposition camp. Before the general election, PAS rapidly expanded its membership with the help of *Harakah*, the party newspaper plus *ceramahs* (or sermons) at Islam mosques, which functioned as the two major sites of popular dissatisfaction with the government, apart from the Internet.[21] "Sales of *Harakah* have jumped from 75,000 in July [1998] to over 300,000 in recent weeks, roughly equal to sales of Malaysia's largest-circulation daily, the pro-UMNO *Utusan Malaysia*."[22] By June 1999, PAS claimed more than six million members.[23] As a consequence, it quadrupled its parliamentary seats and became the leading opposition party for the first time, leaving Chinese-oriented DAP far behind.

The leading party in both the opposition and the government camps was now controlled by Malays for the first time, and thus, the political conflict among Malays would be increasingly more salient than the traditional Chinese versus Malay conflict. The two Malay-controlled parties, PAS and UMNO, are in conflict with each other over issues of economic development and Islamic state. Unlike UMNO pursuing economic development aggressively, PAS is an anti-development party in the sense that its ideal society is not industrial society but rather an agricultural one. "Nik Aziz [PAS leader] declared Kelantan an agricultural-based economy" soon after his election as Chief Minister in 1990. He appeared not to care much about the fact that Kelantan was the poorest state in Malaysia. For example, "He dresses in a loose-fitting robe and shuns the chief minister's official residence. Instead, he lives in his own small, wooden house outside the state capital of Kota Baru."[24] As noted earlier, PAS is also an Islamic party aiming to set up an Islamic state or establish a public sphere according to Islamic principles. In contrast, UMNO adopts a policy line of selective Islamization. Deputy Prime Minister Abdullah Badawi once said that "the Islamic label is not as important as efforts to enhance the Islamic faith and implement developmental programs .... The government's priority is to develop Muslims because this will indirectly boost the image of Islam."[25]

Some observers noted that the surge of Islamic and antidevelopment PAS in the 1999 election might be dangerous for political stability.[26] But one can as well argue that political elite consensus actually increased after the economic crisis. First, as Tengku Razaleigh noted, the 1999 election was the first time that PAS cooperated with non-Muslim parties.[27] After the economic and Anwar crises and the split in UMNO, PAS strategically moderated their positions to forge a united front with DAP against their common opponent. In particular, not only did PAS allow its fundamental principle of setting up an Islamic state to be dropped in the common opposition manifesto, as noted earlier, but also the PAS leader, Nik Aziz, said that his party was willing to accept a non-Muslim Prime Minister, even one from Chinese-oriented DAP. According to Nik Aziz, Islam does not specify the ethnicity of a prime minister.[28]

Second, Keadilan did not claim to embody the true UMNO spirit, unlike a former UMNO splinter party, Semangat 46. Keadilan tried to keep itself detached from UMNO by moving away from UMNO policy positions. By contrast, in 1995, Semangat 46 claimed that it embodied the founding spirit of UMNO. Moreover, it only formed one bilateral coalition with DAP and another coalition with PAS without either party's moderation.[29] Yet, in 1999, Keadilan successfully bridged the opposition alliance between DAP and PAS that moderated their respective positions.

Finally, even though competition for parliamentary seats became more intense in the wake of the economic crisis, the power struggles had already been tamed by election day. It is true that the number of uncontested seats plunged from 11 to 1, and vote differences between the winner and the runner-up decreased in 72 percent of all parliamentary districts. However, this intensified competition did not necessarily mean decreased elite consensus. Key elite players chose not to enflame the election to a disrupting level. They instead carefully arranged election nominations so that the "giant killers" of the opposition camp would not be pitted against "big names" of BN. Moreover, Anwar and another especially controversial figure, Harun Din, who was a PAS central committee member and former Universiti Kebangsaan Malaysia professor, and who once argued for separation of the state of Perlis from the federation, did not stand for election at all. Furthermore, Anwar's wife and Keadilan President, Wan Azizah, chose to stand in Permatang Pauh, Anwar's former constituency and the least provocative of the three constituencies that she could choose. She specifically decided not to lock horns with Mahathir in his constituency, Kubang Pasu. She also discarded Lembah Pantai, which was a BN stronghold in Kuala Lumpur.[30]

More flexible ethnic voting after the crisis

Moving from the elite realignment to mass voting behavior, I noted in Table 6.1 that at the aggregate level about 8.5 percent of voters deserted BN and voted for the opposition in 1999. This loss did not itself seem to pose a serious challenge to the governing coalition or to imply an important shift in the political cleavage structure. However, if we look at district-level voting behavior, we get a different picture. We find, in fact, that the elite realignment was accompanied by a significant change in Malaysia's rigid ethnic voting.

To see how the economic crisis affected the rigid ethnic voting, I first show how many voters defected from BN and voted for the opposition in each electoral district and also how this defection was related to their ethnic identities, using district-level data.[31] To answer these questions, I narrow the cases to include only Peninsular Malaysia. The two island states, Sarawak and Sabah, are excluded because their ethnic compositions and political competitions are quite different from those of states on the peninsula. Both island states have tiny populations of ethnic Chinese and Indians. Parties other than the three peninsula parties play important roles in the two island states, and PAS and DAP are not significant there. Additionally, I focus on the two largest ethnic groups, Malays and ethnic Chinese, since Indian and other minor ethnic populations are not significant at the district level. In Peninsular Malaysia, the percentage of Malays in the district total population is inversely related to the Chinese population in the same electoral district (Figure 6.1). Also note that the Malaysian electoral system is single-member plurality rule as in South Korea.

Having said this, the defection rate from BN, or more technically, the majority shift from BN in an electoral district (Y) is calculated as follows: $Y = W_{99} \frac{Majority_{99}}{V_{99}} - W_{95} \frac{Majority_{95}}{V_{95}}$. In this equation, W_{99} (or W_{95}), which stands for the district winner in 1999 (or in 1995), has a score of 1 if BN won, and −1 if BN lost. V_{99} (or V_{95}) denotes the district vote total in 1999 (or in 1995). $Majority_{99}$ (or $Majority_{95}$) represents the absolute value of the vote difference between district winner and runner-up in 1999 (or in 1995). BN was either winner or runner-up. The value of this variable Y ranges from −2 to 2. If its value is positive, BN's weighted vote majority in 1999 increased or, alternatively, the opposition's weighted vote majority decreased. If its value is negative, BN's weighted vote majority in 1999 decreased, or, alternatively, the opposition's weighted vote majority increased. A value of 0 means that BN's weighted majority (or, alternatively, the opposition's weighted majority) neither increased nor decreased.

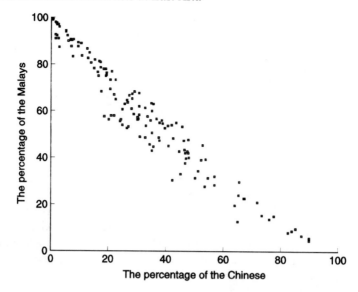

Figure 6.1 The Malay–Chinese proportion in 144 Peninsula Malaysia parliamentary districts.

Source: "Election Results," *New Straits Times,* 1 December 1999.

Figure 6.2 is a scatter plot of the majority shifts from BN in all 144 districts in Peninsular Malaysia according to the percentage of ethnic Malays in the district total population.[32] The figure shows that BN's weighted majority decreased regardless of ethnic composition in virtually all electoral districts in Peninsular Malaysia. The value of the majority shift from BN was less than 0 in virtually all districts. This means that the election campaign effort by BN to fan Chinese fear of ethnic conflict by recalling the 1969 communal riots and neighboring Indonesia's anti-Chinese actions during the crisis was not as effective as BN hoped.

More important for my purpose, the majority shift from BN shows no linear relation to the percentage of Malays (or Chinese) in districts. Apart from a few positive shifts, the loss of BN's weighted vote majority was greatest where the Malays and Chinese were well-mixed or where the population of Malays was neither far greater nor overwhelmingly smaller than the Chinese population. By contrast, where the Malay population was noticeably greater or smaller than the Chinese population, the loss of BN's weighted vote majority remained smallest. In fact, a statistical test shows that a quadratic regression model proves quite significant, and its two regression coefficients are also statistically significant (Table 6.2).

Apart from the fact that ethnically well-mixed constituencies facilitated greater numbers of interactions between ethnic groups, we may explain the quadratic change of BN's weighted majority by the gravity of economic crisis, that is, how hard a particular constituency was hit by the economic crisis. Most of the

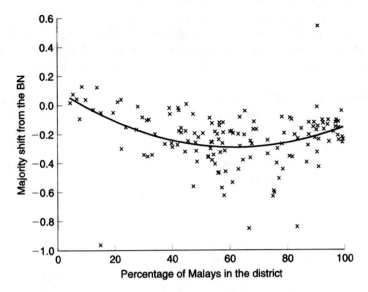

Figure 6.2 Ethnic identity and majority shift from the National Front in the 1999 Malaysian general election (N = 144).

Source: "Election Results," *New Straits Times*, 1 December 1999; and *Bernama*, http://www. bernama.com.my/election.

Table 6.2 Quadratic regression of the majority shift from the National Front (BN)

Model: $Y_i = \beta_0 + \beta_1 X_i + \beta_2 X_i^2$,
where Y_i is the majority shift from BN in district i and X_i is the percentage of Malays in the total population of district i.

Results:

Variables	Coefficients (β)	Standard errors	P values
Constant	0.104669	0.067555	0.1235
X	−0.012769*	0.002501	0.0000
X²	0.000102*	2.1354E-05	0.0000

N = 144
F = 13.29153　　　*p* value of F = .0000

Note: *β_1 and β_2 are significant at the 0.01 level.
Source: "Election Results," New Straits Times, 1 December 1999; and *Bernama*, http://www. bernama.com.my/election.

overwhelmingly Malay areas were spared from the economic crisis as their local economies were based on agriculture, which was not much exposed to international market pressures. Prime Minister Mahathir said that "the rural people were not really concerned about economic recovery because 'fortunately for us, the downturn has not affected the people in the villages because they produce their own food. They are not affected by imports."[33] The predominant Chinese areas were also less affected by the crisis as their local economies were less dependent on external financing and government supports and hence more resilient. The Prime Minister also observed that "while everyone was hit by the downturn, the indigenous [Malay] businessmen were hit the most badly with the big corporations they had success-fully set up unable to withstand the burden of debt they carried." He also added that, "The indigenous middle class, small compared to the non-indigenous one, practically disappeared."[34] In short, predominantly Malay or Chinese districts were less affected by the economic crisis, and, consequently, those areas engaged in more rigid ethnic voting than other areas that were ethnically well-mixed and harder hit by the economic crisis. This is why the majority shift from BN bears a quadratic relation to the district Malay population as in Figure 6.2. These district voting outcomes imply that Malay voters tended to detach themselves from BN when hardest hit by the economic crisis. For systematic analysis of the effects of the economic crisis on ethnic voting, we also need constituency-level economic data. Unfortunately, I do not have this sort of data at hand. So, my conclusion that the economic crisis made the previously rigid ethnic voting more fluid can only be tentative pending more statistical data and analysis.

Conclusion

To summarize, first I have observed that the latent conflict between the Malaysian Prime Minister and his former Deputy, Anwar, in the governing elite camp inten-sified because of their policy disagreements about how to cope with the economic crisis. Mahathir perceived the crisis as a serious threat to his lifetime-long goal, raising up the economic status of Bumiputeras. According to him,

> If the country were to give in to the IMF, it will stop the social engineering process implemented by the government to bridge the gap among the races through the New Economic Policy and order that subsidy given to the people be terminated.[35]

In contrast, Anwar viewed the crisis as an opportunity to review the current policies and to get rid of corruption and collusion between policymakers and economic actors in the government-sponsored economic growth. Subsequently, the Anwar group was expelled from the governing elite and came to align itself with established opposition groups in the form of a loose election coalition that called for major reforms. Yet, unlike other reform movements, the primary bene-ficiary of this reform movement was not those who initiated it, Anwar and his allies, but another Malay-dominated and more radical Islamic party, PAS, which became the leading opposition party in parliament for the first time after the 1999 election. Consequently, the Malaysian political landscape became dominated by two Malay parties. This outcome, that is, the upsurge of Malay–Malay conflicts, would help to lessen the salience of inter-ethnic elite and mass conflicts. The weakening of political conflict between the different ethnic communities was corroborated by the fact that the status of Malay-dominated UMNO in the ruling coalition became significantly weakened, so that it had to rely on other BN component parties for legislative and constitutional actions.

Second, the rise of PAS and the consequent power struggle between UMNO and PAS did not mean a decrease in elite consensus, but rather very likely an increase in elite consensus. This was because PAS's electoral victory was possible only after it abandoned or greatly reduced its rigid Islamic goals; moreover, PAS's further advance in elections, presumably, requires further moderating its Islamic principles.

Third, Malay voters showed that they are willing to desert UMNO or BN during a crisis, regardless of their ethnic identity. My analysis of their voting behavior, using district-level data, shows that their voting is, in fact, quite flexible.

Finally, whether the burgeoning political realignment will flourish depends, among other factors, on the course that Keadilan takes in the power struggle between UMNO and PAS. It is virtually impossible for Keadilan to survive without joining forces one or the other side because the Anwar group's popular support is so widely distributed across the country. This wide distribution of a small party's vote is a clear, possibly fatal, disadvantage in a single-member plurality system as Malaysia is. In fact, the overall support rate for Keadilan was not much different from that for PAS, but the resulting parliamentary seats were markedly different between the two parties (27 for PAS and 5 for Keadilan). Considering the wide distribution of popular support for the Anwar group in a single-member district system, Keadilan will have to seek a stronger coalition with other opposition parties, most likely, DAP, unless it opts to rejoin UMNO and seek reform from inside the governing party.

South Korea

Corporate bankruptcies and the feeble rule of law at the onset of the currency crisis

South Korea was hit by the Asian currency crisis at a time when its economy had already been weakened by a series of bankruptcies of major industrial groups, or chaebols, including Hanbo and Kia. In January 1997, the Hanbo group, the number 14 chaebol, went bankrupt after an over-leveraged investment in the steel industry. Two months later, another chaebol, Sammi, which ranked 26th, collapsed. In another month, the 19th largest chaebol, Jinro, joined the series of bankruptcies. This was followed by yet another collapse of the 34th largest chaebol, Daenong, in May 1997, and other two well-known companies in June. The dominos of collapsing chaebols culminated in the bankruptcy of Kia, one of the three automobile makers and the eighth ranked chaebol, in July. All these were but a part of tens of thousands of bankruptcies (Table 6.3) during 1997. It is worth noting that all these collapses occurred despite overall prospects for continuing Korean economic growth, and for a decreasing current account deficit in 1997.[36]

Table 6.3 Bankruptcies in Korea before the currency crisis

Year/quarter	1996	1997(1/4)	1997(2/4)	1997(3/4)	1997(4/4)	1997
Number	11,589	3,443	3,790	3,834	6,101	17,268

Source: Yonhap Annual (in Korean), vol. 18 (Seoul, 1998), 203.

The East Asian economic crisis also hit South Korea when the term of President Kim Young Sam was nearing its end and when he suffered from a lame-duck status. Competing political groups had begun to regroup for the coming presidential election and were paying less attention to the looming regional currency crisis. Kim Jong Pil, whom Kim Young Sam had sidelined despite their earlier power-sharing agreement, deserted the governing Democratic Liberal Party and formed his own party in 1995. This was a move to prepare for the 1996 parliamentary election, with a longer-term view to playing an independent role in the 1997 presidential election. Given the solid regional divisions after the 1987 democratic transition, it was impossible for Kim Jong Pil to take executive power under the existing presidential system. The reason was that he came from one of the smallest regions. He was thus a diehard proponent of a parliamentary system, even though he had been one of the masterminds of the 1960 coup that toppled the only parliamentary system in Korea's history. After his defection from the governing party, he now turned to Kim Dae Jung's opposition camp. In return for his support for Kim Dae Jung's presidential bid, Kim Jong Pil secured an open agreement from Kim Dae Jung in November. Under this agreement, which was not related to any socioeconomic issues, Kim Dae Jung promised to change the governmental system in the middle of his presidency, split cabinet portfolios equally with Kim Jong Pil's people, and give the position of Prime Minister to Kim Jong Pil's party. Kim Dae Jung did not want to stand any chance of losing the coming election because this was certain to be his last (and fourth) presidential bid. Consequently, he reached the agreement with his old enemy during the struggle for democracy.

After Kim Jong Pil's defection in 1995, the governing DLP ended up as a loose coalition of some former followers of Roh Tae Woo and Chun Doo Hwan, along with the Kim Young Sam supporters. Once Roh and Chun were arrested in December 1995, the DLP was renamed the New Korea Party to signal a break with them. In January 1996, Kim Young Sam brought Yi Hoi Chang, a former Prime Minister, into the governing party as campaign manager for the April parliamentary election, believing that Yi would boost Kim's declining reform image. Yi managed to get himself appointed as party chairperson in March 1997. Subsequently, there occurred serious infighting with other Kim Young Sam men including Kim's one-time hidden candidate for the governing party's presidential candidacy, Lee In Je, during the run up to the New Korea Party's nominating convention. Yi successfully won its nomination in an open contest that was held under a majority run-off system in July 1997. Lee In Je, who was the runner-up in the contest, defected in September to run as a third-party candidate.[37]

In short, when the Asian currency crisis hit Korea, its economy was already weak, and political elites were busy jockeying for position in the forthcoming presidential election. The coalition between Kim Dae Jung and Kim Jong Pil and the defection of Lee In Je from the governing party after his defeat at its nominating convention suggested that the elites were not yet habituated to the existing game rules. Their commitment to the rules was only conditional on their likelihood of winning, and thus, the rule of law was not yet established. The jockeying also showed that elite realignments were not guided by socioeconomic policy agreements or disagreements.

Post-crisis regional political cleavages and elite maneuvers

Once the regional currency crisis greatly aggravated the domestic corporate and banking weaknesses, especially after the Hong Kong stock market's plunge in late October, the government in Seoul, after some initial hesitation, decided to resort to the IMF for an emergency rescue fund on November 21. Five days later, the official presidential election campaign began. Kim Dae Jung initially responded to the IMF rescue program by saying that, if elected president, he would renegotiate the terms with the IMF. Later, he abandoned this stance and joined the other two major candidates in accepting the IMF package. In the largely three-way election, Kim won with 40.3 percent of the popular vote, trailed by Yi Hoi Chang (38.7%), and Lee In Je (19.2%). Among the three main candidates, there was no notable disagreement about how to implement the IMF program, although they disavowed responsibility for the currency crisis.

This section discusses how the economic crisis affected South Korea's rigid regional political cleavage, which had been the most important determinant of election outcomes since 1987. As noted in Chapter 3, the voters that came from the largest and second largest regions, Kyongsang and Cholla, whose combined population accounts for somewhere between 50 percent and 70 percent of the total population, tended to show strongest regional attachments in their voting after the democratic transition.[38] Voters that came from Chungchong, Kim Jong Pil's birthplace, showed a moderate extent of regional attachment. Voters whose birthplace was Seoul, Kyonggi, Kangwon, Cheju, or North Korea were least affected by regional attachments. My analysis here focuses on those who came from Cholla or Kyongsang, wherever they live.[39]

According to a post-election opinion survey ($n = 1195$), 93 percent of Kim Dae Jung's supporters in 1992 who were born in the southwest region, Cholla, continued to vote for him in 1997, while 69 percent of Kim's non-Cholla supporters in 1992 voted again for him in 1997. These two rates were not significantly different from the corresponding figures of 1992, 93 percent and 65 percent (Table 6.4). Meanwhile, 70 percent of the Kyongsang region's natives who had voted for Kim Young Sam in 1992 supported his party in 1997, although the New Korea Party (NKP) tried to keep some distance from Kim during the campaign by renaming itself the Grand National Party (GNP). Fifty-four percent of Kim's non-Kyongsang supporters in 1992 also remained loyal to the NKP or

Table 6.4 Regional voting in the 1997 Korean presidential election

		1992	*1997*
Kim Dae Jung	Cholla natives	96%	93%
	Non-Cholla natives	65	69
Kim Young	Kyongsang natives	68	70
Sam/Yi Hoi Chang	Non-Kyongsang natives	53	54

Source: Institute for Korean Election Studies, *Korean Election Study, 1997: the Fifteenth Presidential Election* (in Korean), codebook (Seoul, 1998).

its successor, the GNP. These two rates were not significantly different from those in 1992, which were 68 and 53 percent, respectively.[40] These steady voting patterns mean that the economic crisis in 1997, taken by itself, did not affect the rigidity of regional voting in Korea, although most respondents in the same survey thought that the currency crisis and attendant inflation were the most important issues in the election.

The small effect of the crisis on the rigidity of the regional political cleavage in Korea was due largely to the fact that those who carried the strongest regional attachment, Cholla natives, were supporters of Kim Dae Jung's opposition party, which bore little responsibility for the crisis. In the above-mentioned survey, 54 percent of respondents thought that the governing party, NKP, was responsible for the crisis, whereas 41 percent said that no party was. Given this, it is not surprising that the crisis induced few Kim Dae Jung's regional supporters to defect from him. So long as the most solid regional lock (Cholla) was not dissolving, Kyongsang voters had no strong incentive to defect from their own regionally dominant party, especially when the destructive socioeconomic effects of the crisis had yet to be fully felt. Yi was not a native of Kyongsang and he tried to keep some distance from Kim Young Sam, but he was still believed to lead a political party that was the most reasonable choice for those Kyongsang natives who disliked Kim Dae Jung and his party.

Yet, over the longer term, the crisis could be expected to influence voters from Cholla and Kyongsang, depending on how Kim Dae Jung implemented the IMF program for economic reforms, since this program was blind to regional identities. To assess this longer-term effect, it is necessary to look at the parliamentary election in April 2000. However, we need to take some precautions in reading the effect of the crisis on regional voting from the 2000 election results. The 2000 election was held when the economy was already recovering. All major macroeconomic indicators by then showed that South Korea was exiting from the crisis, except for a still high rate of unemployment. In addition, right before the election, the government made the shocking announcement that Kim Dae Jung and Kim Jung Il would hold a North–South Korea summit. This was to be the first ever meeting between North and South Korean leaders, and the announcement was believed to favor the government in the 2000 election. Finally, I do not have appropriate individual survey data and must rely on the aggregate election outcomes for my analysis. All these considerations mean that it is difficult to disentangle the effects of the economic crisis on the 2000 election from the effects of other events.

This said, the most notable aspect of the 2000 election was that, in Kyongsang, Yi Hoi Chang's opposition party took all seats except one independent seat.[41] This was the first time since 1987 that one party completely captured the region, and many pundits quickly concluded that regional voting was, accordingly, stronger than before. Arguably, many Kyongsang voters that previously engaged in regional voting were all the more inclined to do so after the Kim Dae Jung government's implementation of the belt-tightening IMF package. There is some truth to this argument.

But an alternative explanation for the nearly complete victory of Yi's party in Kyongsang is that voters who detached themselves from their regionally dominant party did not vote, leaving only those voters whose old antipathy toward Kim Dae Jung was reinforced by his economic measures to register their anger against the Kim government at the polls. In other words, die-hard regional voters were over-represented in the election due to a lower turnout by post-crisis defectors from regional voting habits. We see this trend in the lowest national participation rate, 57.2 percent, in parliamentary elections since 1987. Although the turnout continued to decline after 1987, widespread alienation after the economic crisis was central to a large marginal drop in turnout, 6.7 percent.[42]

The fact that defections from the regionally dominant party in Kyongsang were lower among *actual* voters than among *total registered* voters supports this alternative thesis. It is true that, in all four Kyongsang areas (Taegu, Pusan, and North and South Kyongsang), Yi's opposition party actually earned greater proportions of votes in 2000 than in 1996; hence, the economic crisis arguably reinforced old regional voting patterns. But support rates for Yi's opposition party in all four areas were also much greater among *actual* voters than among *total registered* voters. The marginal increases in the party's support rate among *actual* voters were 38 percent in Taegu, 18 percent in North Kyongsang, 5 percent in Pusan, and 4 percent in South Kyongsang. By contrast, the marginal increases among *total registered* voters were 19, 9, 0, and 0 percent in the four areas, respectively.[43] This means that defectors from Yi's opposition party were underrepresented in the final election results because of their lower turnout rates. The same tendency can also be observed in Cholla where the average defection rate for Kim's governing party was lower among *actual* voters than among *total registered* voters. The party's average support rate in the region dropped by 6 percent among *actual* voters, but it decreased by 8 percent among *total registered* voters. In other words, defectors from the regionally dominant party in Cholla were also under-represented in the election outcomes because they simply did not turn out.[44]

Previously regional, but now disaffected voters simply abstained because there was no serious policy-related partisanship between the established parties in their region. Even after the economic crisis, Korean political elites did not actively campaign for support from regional constituencies of their opponents. Instead, they worked hard to consolidate their own precrisis regional constituencies. For instance, Kim Dae Jung's party spent more money in Cholla, but not in Kyongsang, than did the opposition party. Although the governing elite group expected some of its traditional regional supporters to defect, the magnitude of this defection was not expected to be large enough to threaten majority status in safe regional districts. Nonetheless, they spent more money on their safe havens during the election campaign than did the opposition elite. This was also true of Yi's opposition party in its safe districts. In sum, competing political elites still did not try all that hard to appeal to the precrisis regional constituencies of opposing parties.[45]

In short, the economic crisis did not demolish Korea's regional voting cleavage. It seemed to reinforce the antipathy in Kyongsang toward Kim Dae Jung and his political party, because it was the Kim government that implemented, though it did not incur, the painful IMF program. However, the 2000 parliamentary election results also showed that many voters who previously engaged in regional voting were disenchanted and began to detach themselves from their regionally dominant party. Although they were not terribly large in numbers, they may well constitute a new pool of voters to whom policy-oriented political elites can appeal effectively. For the moment, these people simply do not vote.

Strengthening the state, dissolving the chaebols, and continuing wealth concentration

There are a number of studies of the Kim Dae Jung government's performance after he in effect took executive power even before being inaugurated as president in February 1998.[46] The following paragraph is one of the best summaries, which was written in 1999.[47]

> By February 1999, the first anniversary of his inauguration, it seemed as if the liquidity crisis had been resolved and exchange-rate stability had been restored. A record rise in the current accounts surplus in 1998 to $ 40 billion alleviated fears that there would be a shortage of foreign exchange, leading to a recurrence of the currency crisis. By the middle of February, the Korean won, which had reached a low of 1,965 to the dollar, was trading at 1,181, moving closer to the pre-crisis rate of around 900. In reaction to this news, international credit agencies raised Korea's sovereign ratings, the risk assessments assigned to the obligations of central governments, to investment grade in early 1999. The domestic economy shows signs of recovery due to falling interest rates. Individual output began to rise in the fourth quarter of 1998 after four consecutive quarters of negative growth. Korea has carried out the structural reform program that it agreed to with the International Monetary Fund(IMF). By February 1999, the first stages of labor and banking reforms had been completed, and the first stage of corporate reform was drawing to a close.

It is no doubt that the Kim government in Korea was the most successful implementer of the IMF program among the five crisis-hit countries. "Korea has been exceptionally steadfast in implementing the IMF program. It has far exceeded initial expectations of the IMF and the international financial community by carrying out various measures in advance of the agreed schedule."[48]

This remarkable achievement in South Korea reflected its high precrisis level of elite consensus, which surpassed that among elites in the other countries. Elites in South Korea were not as fragmented as in Thailand, and they certainly were not as divided as in Indonesia. Most notably, Korea's new democracy successfully and peacefully got rid of one of the common threats to democracy, that of a military coup, by the time the Asian economic crisis engulfed the country, as noted in Chapter 3. The experience of resolving the military's political involvement in a peaceful and incremental way, and the consequent strengthening of elite consensus had spill-over effects in other arenas. For example, it is notable that the Korean opposition did not have any serious disagreements with the Kim Dae Jung government about implementing the IMF program. Instead, they merely criticized the government for incompleteness or inconsistency in its implementation efforts. In particular, the labor and financial reform laws that were passed in parliament after the currency crisis were the same bills that the Kim Young Sam government had drafted and that Kim Dae Jung's opposition party had blocked while in opposition during 1996 and 1997. There was no reason for the old governing party to oppose these reform bills when in opposition. It appears that there was a comprehensive consensus among the elite that structural reforms were indispensable. This consensus was largely due to a shift in the previous opposition party's attitudes once in government. Notably, once in power, Kim Dae Jung turned out to be a neoliberal that believed in free markets and small government, though he was previously viewed as a social democrat. Once in power, he virtually ceased appealing to lower class segments including labor unions, for support.

Yet, it must also be said that the policy consensus among Korean elites was not echoed in the wider society. The prevalent neoliberal policy line did not provide the established political parties a *raison d'etre*, and it did not resonate in their bases of mass support. Nor is the elite consensus so consolidated that it is unlikely to shift at some point when popular sentiments go strongly against the neoliberal policy line. Moreover, the Korean elite still lacks sufficient differentiation to become truly consensual. Consensus does not mean policy unanimity or silent opposition to policies. Consensus presumes a significant amount of structural differentiation and, based on this, meaningful opposition. From this perspective, the most worrisome trends after the crisis have been the expansion of the state and consequently the further blurring of the private and public boundary, as well as the further concentration of wealth.

The South Korean state steadily weakened in the face of ever more vocal business sectors between the 1987 democratic transition and the regional crisis ten years later. One of the most striking demonstrations of this was Chung Ju Young's bid for power in the 1992 presidential election. Chung, founder of the biggest chaebol, Hyundai, entered the presidential race to oppose the state's traditional intervention in business activities. Yet, during the currency crisis, state power, with the heavy leverage of the IMF over other domestic business actors, increased. This began when virtually the whole banking sector was placed under government control. Nine of 30 merchant banks, which were hit the most seriously by the currency crisis because of their poor management of short-term foreign borrowings, were suspended early in December 1997 and placed under the direct control of the Ministry of Finance and Economy. In January 1998, the government successfully negotiated with foreign bank creditors to turn some 25 billion dollar short-term private debts into long-term ones by offering government guarantees and higher interest rates. These debts were what the private actors, mostly merchant banks, owed to foreign private banks. Yet, the government came forward to cover the debts, under the exaggerated threat of sovereign default in international financial markets. By summer 1999, of the 30 merchant banks that had been operating in 1997, 16 had been closed, two merged, one suspended, and only 11 were still operating. The assets and debts of the closed banks were transferred to a bridging merchant bank, Hanaram, which was placed under government control. In addition to specialized and development banks already under its control, the government also took over commercial banks. It nationalized Korea First Bank and Seoul Bank in January 1998. Still two other major banks merged and were nationalized in September. Most of the other commercial banks that were not yet nationalized had the government as a major shareholder (Table 6.5). For bank restructuring, the government spent 51.1 trillion won by August 1999, which was equivalent to 11. 5 percent of the 1998 Gross National Income (GNI) and surpassed the shareholders' equity in the top five chaebols in 1997, 46.9 trillion won.

Once the banking sector was placed under its control, the government was in a position to exert unchallenged influence over the restructuring of indebted corporations. The average debt ratio in manufacturing was 396.3 percent in 1997. The top 5 chaebols' debt ratio in the same year was 470.2 percent, and the top 6–30 chaebols' debt ratio was 521.5.[49] The government's bank control may not be permanent, since it wants to dispose of its shares after the NPLs have been cleaned up. Nonetheless, the government does not have a long-term master plan to dispose of its massive banking shares. Nor do political elites have a consensus on how to dispose of them. Moreover, the government has been pressuring more banks to merge with the aim of creating one or two banks of global magnitude. It is much more difficult to dispose of the government's shares in such a mammoth bank. The basic dilemma is that other than chaebols are incapable of obtaining a control share of such a mammoth bank, while industrial chaebols' banking control will greatly exacerbate the concentration of wealth. At present, the government upholds the long-established principle of separation of industrial and banking capital.

Along with the rigid regional cleavages and the extensive state intervention, the concentration of national assets in a few industrial oligarchs had the effect of blocking extensive structural differentiation or pluralism. Although political dictatorship ended in 1987, economic monopoly or oligopoly was sustained or

Table 6.5 Government stake in Korean commercial banks before and after the crisis (per cent)

Banks	After crisis	Before crisis
Korea First Bank*	93.8	0
Seoul Bank	93.8	0
Peace Bank	n.a.	0
Chohung Bank	91	.3
Foreign Exchange Bank	33.6	47.9
Hanvit Bank	94.8	0
Hanmi (Koram) Bank	34.7	n.a.
Hana Bank	57.5	0
Kookmin Bank	21.5	15.16
Housing Bank	49.6	22.38
Sinhan Bank	25.0	0

Source: Organization for Economic Cooperation and Development, *OECD Economic Surveys: Korea 1998–1999* (in Korean) (Paris: OECD, 1999) and Departments of Public Relations in the respective banks.

Note: Jungmin Kim in the FEER Seoul Bureau obtained the precrisis figures on behalf of me. Minor provincial-level banks were excluded from the table. Terms of investment for the sale of 51 percent stake of the KFB(*) to New Bridge Capital were agreed in September 1999.

rather strengthened, as seen in Chapter 3. The top five big business families accounted for 30 percent of the national assets right before the economic crisis, and the top thirty took about 46 percent.

The Kim Dae Jung government initially championed voluntary and market-oriented corporate restructuring, and it focused policy efforts on the issues of corporate governance such as transparency and accountability. Decentralizing national assets or dissolving the chaebol system was not on the government's initial economic reform agenda. President-elect Kim Dae Jung held a private meeting with the top four chaebol owners in January 13, 1998,[50] and they agreed to do their best to achieve the five basic goals of corporate restructuring such as enhancing transparency and accountability in corporate governance and eliminating mutual guarantees and excessive business diversification.

However, the voluntary or market-oriented corporate restructuring turned out to be unsuccessful. By June 1998, the government began to be impatient with the sluggish corporate restructuring and finally intervened in the process. On June 18, it announced that 55 nonviable corporations were to exit from the market. At first, without government intervention, creditor banks had selected out only 14 nonviable corporations, and none of the 14 belonged to the top five chaebols. Despite the repeated government announcements that corporate restructuring would take place between creditor banks and debtors, banks tried to find out what the government truly wanted before acting. This was largely due to the fact that the banking sector was not independent and did not have full responsibility for corporate restructuring.

After the announcement of nonviable corporations on June 18, the government speeded up the restructuring process. A week later, it brought 210 financial institutions under an accord of the Corporate Restructuring Agreement (CRA). This agreement provided for a procedure for debt workouts. This workout framework was applied to all but the top-five chaebols. At the end of October 1998, 67 companies were placed under the workout program, including 41 chaebol affiliates. Yet, the government did not apply the CRA framework to the top five chaebols. They were, instead, separately required to submit improved Capital Structure Improvement Plans (CSIPs) to their lead banks. Under this framework, after the top five chaebols agreed on CSIPs with their lead banks, the banks would review the possibility of bringing the chaebols' loss-making affiliates into the debt workout process.[51] In short, the government looked very hesitant to workout any major top five chaebol affiliate.

The preferential treatment of the top five chaebols made their corporate restructuring only sluggish. While all other businesses appeared drowning amidst the currency crisis, the big five chaebols, particularly, Hyundai, seemed to expand even though they were also heavily indebted. This made it difficult for the government to build a solid public consensus on economic reforms, especially, labor reform. "So far [by December 1998], some 20 thousands of medium- and small-sized businesses went bankrupt. Half the 6-30 top chaebols were virtually dissolved. By contrast, the voluntary restructuring of the big five chaebols were not as satisfactory."[52]

The government finally hammered out another agreement with the big five chaebols on December 7, 1998. This agreement basically reiterated the key points of the January 1998 one, but it now brought up a concrete action plan. Subsequently, the big five's debt ratio was reduced to 302 percent in June 1999 from 386 percent at the end of 1998 (Table 6.6). Yet, this decrease was not due to a cut in their debt, but to an increase in their shareholders' equity. This means that their total assets rather increased, and, consequently, the national assets were further concentrated. In fact, Table 6.7 shows that the concentration of national assets had steadily increased before the crisis, and this trend was not reversed even after the economic crisis. Yet, the longer-term effect of the economic crisis on the concentration of national assets is not easy to ascertain, given the government's inconsistent policies about corporate restructuring and the continuing collapses of chaebols including the second-ranked Daewoo.[53]

Conclusion

To summarize, though we still have yet to see the longer-term effects of the economic crisis, based on the two years that followed it, I have argued that regional linkages between the Korean political elites and voters were not fundamentally disrupted. The 2,000 parliamentary election showed that the political elites still worked hard to consolidate their regional constituencies instead of appealing to opposing elites' constituencies. Second, despite the most successful implementation of the IMF-mandated reform program among the five crisis-hit

Table 6.6 Top five chaebols' debt ratio and shareholders' equity after the crisis

	1997 (year-end)	1998 (year-end)	June 99
Debt ratio (%).	470.2	386.0	302.2
Debt (trillion won)	220.4	225.1	222.7
Shareholders' equity (trillion won)	46.9	58.3	73.7

Source: Sangin Hwang, Yeunjong Wang, and Sengbung Yi, *Korean Economy under the IMF Program* (in Korean), vol. 2 (Seoul: KIIEP,1999), 166.

Table 6.7 Chaebols' assets as a proportion of national assets after the crisis (per cent)

	1994	1995	1996	1997	1998
Top five chaebols	23.39	25.42	26.98	29.92	31.61
Top ten chaebols	32.42	33.87	35.64	36.29	38.57
Top 30 chaebols	41.56	44.86	46.61	46.25	47.79

Source: Seung No Choi, *Big Businesses in Korea, 1999* (in Korean) (Seoul: Free Enterprise Center. 1999), 23.

countries, the Korean reform process generated a stronger state sector that the private sector could not check and balance. This was largely due to the state's virtual control of the banking sector. Given the credit crunch and disappearance of other sources of credit, virtually all the indebted private businesses had to rely on the government for their survival. With the state's increased power, the private sector's vulnerability to government policy shifts increased. Finally, the differential corporate restructuring of the top five and other chaebols had the short-term effect of concentrating national assets in still fewer hands. Along with strengthening state power, this enhanced concentration of wealth disfavors further elite differentiation.

On the other hand, it is true that the belt-tightening IMF program led some previously regional voters to defect from their regionally dominant parties. Additionally, the successful implementation of the IMF program increased the transparency of corporate management and, consequently, made corrupt business-government linkages easier to detect. Despite the greater concentration of national assets, moreover, the chaebol system was heavily damaged. Many chaebols collapsed, and any remaining legitimacy of the system all but evaporated. Finally, despite my rather pessimistic portrayal of post-crisis political economy in Korea, I do not see any immediate systematic threat to Korean democracy and do not deny that the longer-term effects of the crisis may enhance elite cooperation and consensus.

7 Conclusions

Most studies of the Asian economic crisis deal with its economic or political consequences in a single country. Even when they cover several countries, they are edited volumes that deal with various aspects of the crisis without a common theoretical framework.[1] Consequently, the existing literature about the Asian economic crisis lacks a systematic, cross-national, and comparative analysis.[2]

In addition, the greater portion of the literature focuses on economic issues such as how the crisis originated, why particular countries like Taiwan and Singapore were largely unaffected, why some countries turned to the IMF for help while others, like Malaysia, generally did not, and how the crisis affected regional economic cooperation through ASEAN and APEC. Even when the existing literature deals with the more political aspects of the crisis, it discusses the process of economic (i.e., corporate, financial, and labor) reform, or it addresses the issues of why some countries adopted a neoliberal economic policy regime and how successful they were in implementing neoliberal economic policies. In other words, the existing literature is primarily oriented toward specific economic policies and policymaking process. Consequently, it pays little attention to the direct effects of the economic crisis on political elites.

Yet, it is *political* elites that ultimately take the responsibility for making and implementing economic policies. Even when it comes to *economic* crisis, *political* elites decide on how to handle it. Moreover, political elites cannot be viewed as a constant variable. They are seriously affected by economic crisis, and, consequently, many of them rise and fall with it. Crisis-induced circulations and realignments of political elites, in turn, affect the direction and success of economic reform. The scant attention in the literature on the Asian economic crisis to its direct effects on political actors is all the more surprising because many pundits view the crisis as having originated in political elites' corrupt links to the business sector.

Unlike other studies, this volume has attempted a systematic and comparative analysis of the direct effects of the Asian economic crisis on political elites. Although I have discussed how political elites responded to the crisis and the economic policies they adopted, I have been primarily interested in how the crisis affected political elites themselves. More specifically, while assuming that elite cooperation is the key to overcoming economic crisis and maintaining regime stability, I have argued that the effects of economic crisis on political stability are not monolithic. The effects vary depending on elite configurations or modes of political elite behavior that exist at the onset of economic crisis.

On the other hand, I have also argued that elite configurations themselves are not fixed but may instead be transformed by economic crisis. This volume has examined the elite transformations that took place during and after the Asian economic crisis. In particular, I have tried to delineate specific conditions for the transformation of nonconsensual elites into consensual ones. By addressing the question of how nonconsensual elites become consensual, I have dealt indirectly with a central question in formal theory, namely, the origins of cooperation.

My key contention has been that different countries take different paths to elite cooperation in the wake of economic crisis, depending on their precrisis elite configurations or modes of operation. A divided elite may take the settlement path to consensus, whereas a fragmented elite may take the convergence path. But not every divided or fragmented elite becomes consensual during or after economic crisis. An elite settlement in a previously divided elite configuration occurs only when the initial balance of power between divided elite groups has been more or less even. If no such balance has existed at the onset of crisis, divided elites remain divided or become fragmented. Similarly, an elite convergence in a previously fragmented elite configuration is more likely when fragmented elite groups are at the outset aligned on a single dominant and linear cleavage line in such a way that there is a nonarbitrary and thus stable center-point toward which they can subsequently converge.

Of the five countries I studied, Indonesia was viewed as having a divided elite in 1997 at the onset of the economic crisis. In this divided configuration, the balance of power clearly favored the governing elite camp, dominated by President Suharto and the military. Opposition elite groups had long been relatively weak and unorganized. Consequently, lacking any power balance, there could be no elite settlement in Indonesia during or after the economic crisis. The military-dominated government collapsed when the international pressures seriously undermined President Suharto's power and thus abruptly tilted the quite uneven balance of power among domestic actors. Combined with this primarily foreign-driven and abrupt change in government, multiple crosscutting cleavages, as well as permissive and open-ended political game rules, fueled elite fragmentation. In short, Indonesia did not satisfy the precondition for an elite settlement when the crisis occurred. Consequently, the country moved toward a highly volatile fragmented elite pattern under the influence of social and institutional factors that made it difficult for political elites to coordinate with each other.

By contrast, Thailand and the Philippines had fragmented elite configurations before the crisis. Yet, neither country had a dominant linear political cleavage line. Consequently, they could not undergo an elite convergence during the crisis. In Thailand specifically, no single political cleavage prevailed before the crisis, even though the old military/anti-military cleavage had been steadily receding. This meant that there was no clear divide between political elite camps vying for executive power. To cope with the Asian economic crisis, Thai elites simply regrouped themselves and put forward a political front that was more acceptable to both the disgruntled public and the demanding international creditors. Chuan Leekpai led this new coalition government that adopted an IMF-style neoliberal policy regime.

Meanwhile, a precrisis political reform movement that had been centered on a constitutional amendment initiative gathered momentum in Thailand during the crisis. Subsequently, a new constitution that included new election rules finally passed in parliament without notable popular upheavals or coup attempts. This was because Thai political elites by and large refrained from mobilizing the masses to serve their factional interests. They avoided holding massive public rallies, calling a new general election, or staging another coup, any of which might have worked as a focal or rallying point to galvanize the discontented masses. Thai elites' collective avoidance of mass mobilizations during the economic crisis contrasted with the marked populist course of action that Filipino elites took during the same period.

In the Philippines before the regional economic crisis occurred, an ethno-linguistic cleavage was apparently the most salient political cleavage, even though its absolute magnitude of importance was not that great because it did not rest on strong and mutually hostile ethno-linguistic identities. Rather, it was rooted in Filipino elites' prevalent patron–client ties to local constituencies, which happened to fall within the boundaries of regionally concentrated linguistic groups. This meant that the precrisis ethno-linguistic cleavage in the Philippines was quite mutable. In other words, there were no insurmountable walls of hatred or animosity among ethno-linguistic groups. This was why fragmented Filipino elites were often able to resort to the relatively undifferentiated mass public ("the people") to reach outcomes in their power struggles. Filipino politics during the crisis was characterized by populist strategies in which fragmented elites tried to prevail over each other by appealing to the public in a variety of ways. In such populist politics, political elites do not compete for public support with concrete policies, and they tend to ignore formal decision making mechanisms and processes.

Of utmost importance to populist politics are public sentiments that override legal and constitutional frameworks. Populism is the opposite of delegative democracy, in which the arbitrary decision making power of presidents and their entourages are foremost. Both types of politics are possible when there are no differentiated political constituencies that bind political elites to a range of public policies or political lines. But neither form of politics, populism or delegative democracy, is conducive to consolidating democracy. For democratic consolidation, the masses need to be demobilized after a democratic transition, and political elites must have considerable autonomy. What the Filipinos call "people's power" cannot lead to stable democracy because it weakens formal institutional mechanisms and processes. It is more likely to lead to mob rule. Populism, incarnating the people as ultimate rulers and arbitrators, characterized constitutional debates at the early stage of the Asian economic crisis in the Philippines, and it strongly colored Estrada's election campaign in the ensuing 1998 presidential election.[3]

If a precrisis mode of elite operation is consensual, it is likely to persist during a crisis. However, there was no case of an established consensual elite configuration among the five countries studied in this volume. But there were two cases of semi-consensual elite configurations at the onset of the crisis: Malaysia and South Korea. The challenging question both pose is under what conditions semi-consensus among elites degenerates, is strengthened, or simply remains unchanged. I have not been able to give a theoretical answer, in part because I have only these two cases from which to generalize. I have sought, instead, to analyze how the semi-consensual elites in South Korea and Malaysia changed during and after the economic crisis. In doing so, I paid particular attention to the extent of elite differentiation in both countries, that is, the functional diversification of elites and their autonomy from the state, in addition to the rigidity of their ties to mass constituencies. I have argued that narrow elite differentiation and rigid political ties between elites and their electoral constituencies were the defining elements of *semi*-consensual elites in Malaysia and South Korea at the onset of the crisis.

I found that Malaysian elites became more consensual as a consequence of the crisis, while South Korean elites underwent no major change in their precrisis configuration. More specifically in Malaysia, the dominant elite coalition, the National Front, was significantly weakened after a crisis-induced split in its core UMNO component, while the two most important opposition elite groups, heading PAS and DAP, moderated their issue positions and began to bridge the divide between them. Moreover, the previously rigid ethnic voting patterns among Chinese and Malays became more fluid. These changes contributed to a greater differentiation of Malaysian elites, less rigid alignments among them, narrowed issue differences, and somewhat less reliable mass constituencies.

In South Korea, by contrast, despite the Kim Dae Jung government's sound macroeconomic performance during the crisis, accompanied by a greater transparency in business–government relations, all but complete government control of the banking sector blurred the rather nebulous boundary between state and society. A main consequence was that the state, which had been substantially weakened during and after Korea's 1987 democratic transition, began to reassert itself, becoming more interventionist through its control of the financial system and the national assets were concentrated in still fewer hands than before. Importantly in Korea, rigid linkages between elites and voters, which are based on primordial regional ties, were not fundamentally disrupted by the economic crisis. This continuation of increasing state power, further concentration of national wealth, and unchanged voter loyalties left Korean elites without the wide differentiation and relative autonomy from the state that are hallmarks of fully consensual elites. At the same time, however, the partial consensus that Korean elites had achieved in 1987 did not weaken significantly in the face of the economic crisis.

When compared with other countries, the semi-consensual elites in Malaysia and South Korea displayed remarkable resilience during the economic crisis and the equally quick recovery from it. Malaysian elites especially were noteworthy in this respect. Of the five countries that this volume studied, Malaysia was the only country that did not experience any change in political regime or in government during the crisis. The political resilience of elites and the rapid economic recoveries in Malaysia and Korea, which surprised other crisis-affected countries in both respects, cannot be explained by political regime type (authoritarian versus democratic), government system (presidential versus parliamentary), parliamentary strength of governing parties, the relative gravity of economic crisis, the intensity of class conflict, corrupt or clean business–government ties, or by economic policies and programs. The two countries had opposite government systems: parliamentary in Malaysia and presidential in South Korea. They also implemented contrasting economic programs: largely Keynesian in Malaysia and IMF-style austerity in South Korea. The relative gravity of economic crisis was also different: South Korea was the second most seriously affected country next to Indonesia, while Malaysia's level of economic crisis was next to the Philippines, the least affected among the five countries. Malaysia's governing coalition controlled a supermajority in parliament, while the Kim Dae Jung government did not enjoy a parliamentary majority at all. South Korea's trade unions were notorious for their militancy, while Malaysia's trade unions were by comparison docile. The Malaysian ruling coalition's ties to the Malay business sector were hardly clean and they were very tight, while Kim Dae Jung and his party were only loosely tied to the dominant business sector because of Kim's precrisis opposition status. What all these contrasts add up to is that the countries had little in common except that they both had semi-consensual elites at the onset of the economic crisis.

Many observers believe that the five countries' vulnerability to external economic shocks was rooted in business–government relations, especially the concentration of economic power, government involvement in banking, industrial policy, and weak liberalization.[4] Neoliberal policies advocated and adopted during the Asian economic crisis were supposed to reduce this economic vulnerability. They have not, however, accomplished this in any clear fashion. For instance, a major irony of the economic crisis in Korea is that the IMF-style neoliberal economic program has led to further concentration of economic power and strengthened government intervention in banking and other businesses. This means that the crisis-hit countries remain vulnerable to another bout of economic crisis. When and if this occurs, its effects on elites will be the key thing to examine. This volume has sought to provide tools for conducting that examination.

Notes

1 Introduction: Economic crises, political elites, and democratic stability

1 Stephan Haggard and Robert R. Kaufman, *The Political Economy of Democratic Transitions* (Princeton, NJ: Princeton University Press, 1995); Mark Kesselman, 'How Should One Study Economic Policy-making?: Four Characters in Search of an Object,' *World Politics* 44 (July 1992): 645–672; and W. Rand Smith, 'International Economy and State Strategies: Recent Work in Comparative Political Economy,' *Comparative Politics* 25 (April 1993): 351–72.
2 Robert D. Putnam, *Making Democracy Work: Civic Traditions in Modern Italy* (Princeton: Princeton University Press, 1993), Chapter 6; Robert H. Bates, 'Contra Contractarianism: Some Reflections on the New Institutionalism,' *Politics and Society* 16 (1988): 387–401; and Elinor Ostrom, *Governing the Commons: The Evolution of Institutions for Collective Action* (New York: Cambridge University Press, 1990).
3 Larry Diamond, ed., *Political Culture and Democracy in Developing Countries* (Boulder, CO: L. Rienner Publishers, 1993); Gabriel A. Almond and Sidney Verba, *The Civic Culture: Political Attitudes and Democracy in Five Nations* (Princeton, NJ: Princeton University Press, 1963); and Putnam, *Making Democracy Work*.
4 John Higley and Richard Gunther, eds., *Elites and Democratic Consolidation in Latin America and Southern Europe* (New York: Cambridge University Press, 1992).
5 Putnam, *Making Democracy Work*, 180.
6 Barry R. Weingast, 'The Political Foundations of Democracy and the Rule of Law,' *American Political Science Review* 91 (June 1997): 258.
7 Michael Burton and John Higley, 'Political Crises and Elite Settlements,' in *Elites, Crises, and the Origins of Regimes*, ed., Mattei Dogan and John Higley (Lanham, MD: Rowman & Littlefield Publishers, 1998); Higley and Gunther, eds., *Elites and Democratic Consolidation*; Dankwart Rustow, 'Transitions to Democracy: Toward a Dynamic Model,' *Comparative Politics* 2 (April 1970): 337–363.
8 Karen L. Remmer, 'The Political Impact of Economic Crisis in Latin America in the 1980s,' *American Political Science Review* 85 (September 1991): 793. Also see her article, 'Debt or Democracy: The Political Impact of the Debt Crisis in Latin America,' in *Debt and Transfiguration?: Prospects for Latin America's Economic Revival*, ed. David Felix (Armonk, NY: M. E. Sharpe, Inc., 1990).
9 Jeffry A. Frieden, *Debt, Development, and Democracy: Modern Political Economy and Latin America, 1965–1985* (Princeton, NJ: Princeton University Press, 1991), 36.
10 Haggard and Kaufman, *The Political Economy of Democratic Transitions*, 7.
11 Ibid., 325.
12 Mancur Olson, 'Rapid Growth as a Destabilizing Force,' *Journal of Economic History* 23 (December 1963): 530.

13 Ibid., 543.
14 Carlos H. Acuna and William C. Smith, 'The Political Economy of Structural Adjustment: The Logic of Support and Opposition to Neoliberal Reform,' in *Latin American Political Economy in the Age of Neoliberal Reform: Theoretical and Comparative Perspectives for the 1990s,* ed., William C. Smith, Carlos H. Acuna, and Eduardo A. Gamarra (Miami, FL: The University of Miami North-South Center, 1994), 40.
15 For example, the bureaucratic authoritarianism model attributes democratic breakdown to economic crisis. Guillermo O'Donnell, *Modernization and Bureaucratic Authoritarianism: Studies in South American Politics* (Berkeley, CA: University of California, 1973).
16 Juan Linz and Alfred Stepan, *Problems of Democratic Transition and Consolidation: Southern Europe, South America, and Post-Communist Europe* (Baltimore, MD: The Johns Hopkins University Press, 1996), 79. A basic assumption of their democratic legitimacy theory is that the stability of democracy relies on its popularity with the masses. This assumption has been disputed. For example, 'political leaders are aware that the rise and fall of democracy in Latin America have corresponded less to the whims of the voting majority than to the concerted opposition of business and military elites.' Karen L. Remmer, 'Democracy and Economic Crisis: The Latin American Experience,' *World Politics* 42 (April 1990): 335.
17 Geddes observes that 'Economic crises threaten the survival of all forms of government, democratic and authoritarian. Military governments are more vulnerable to economic downturns than are other authoritarianisms [personalist and single-party regimes] because poor economic performance is likely to precipitate or worsen splits in the officer corps.' Barbara Geddes, 'What Do We Know about Democratization after Twenty Years?' *Annual Review of Political Science* 2 (1999): 135.
18 Ekkart Zimmermann and Thomas Saalfeld, 'Economic and Political Reactions to the World Economic Crisis of the 1930s in Six European Countries,' *International Studies Quarterly* 32 (1988): 307. For more observations to the same effect, see John Markoff and Silvio R. Duncan Baretta, 'Economic Crisis and Regime Change in Brazil: The 1960s and the 1980s,' *Comparative Politics* (July 1990): 425; and Mark J. Gasiorowski, 'Economic Crisis and Political Regime Change: An Event History Analysis,' *American Political Science Review* 89 (December 1995): 1005.
19 John Higley and Michael Burton, 'Elite Transformation in Democratization's Three Waves,' paper delivered to the International Political Science Association World Congress, Quebec, August 2000.
20 Linz and Stepan, *Problems of Democratic Transition and Consolidation,* 55–65.
21 Burton and Higley, 'Political Crises and Elite Settlements'; Michael Burton, Richard Gunther, and John Higley, 'Introduction: Elite Transformation and Democratic Regimes,' in *Elites and Democratic Consolidation,* ed., John Higley and Richard Gunther, 13–24.
22 Linz and Stepan, *Problems of Democratic Transition and Consolidation,* 61–65; Samuel P. Huntington, *The Third Wave: Democratization in the Late Twentieth Century* (London: University of Oklahoma Press, 1991), 151–161; Adam Przeworski, *Democracy and the Market: Political and Economic Reforms in Eastern Europe and Latin America* (Cambridge, MA: Cambridge University Press, 1991), 67–79. For a similar but more inclusive concept, 'transitions by agreement,' see Josep M. Colomer, *Strategic Transitions: Game Theory and Democratization* (Baltimore, MA: The Johns Hopkins University Press, 2000).
23 Linz and Stephan, *Problems of Democratic Transition and Consolidation,* 61 and 65. Also see Przeworski, *Democracy and the Market,* 66-79.
24 Weingast, 'The Rule of Law.'
25 Ibid., 251.
26 Ibid., 258.

27 Ibid., 252–3 and 259.
28 Przeworski, *Democracy and the Market*, 83–84 (Italics added).
29 Ibid., 87.
30 'Burton, Gunther' and Higley, 'Introduction,' 24–30.
31 Here, the term 'ideology' is used in a very limited sense. It denotes a coherent set of political principles guiding class-based political struggles or policymaking. There are different conceptions of classes. Understanding a class as some sort of qualitative entity that is completely separated from another class is incompatible with my argument. This Marxist understanding of classes does not allow for 'middle classes.' My argument is compatible only with a conception of a class as a kind of quantitative entity whose difference with another class is only a matter of degree in its possession of some social value such as income. Only in this sense of classes is the term 'middle classes' meaningful.
32 For example, Samuel P. Huntington, 'Democracy for the Long Haul,' *Journal of Democracy* 7 (April 1996): 3–13. Even the installation of stable democracy in the form of consociational democracy in an ethnically divided society is feasible only after majority rule is significantly compromised. Arend Lijphart, *Democracies: Patterns of Majoritarian and Consensus Government in Twenty-One Countries* (New Haven, CT: Yale University Press, 1984).
33 An example is Donald L. Horowitz, *Ethnic Groups in Conflict* (Berkeley, CA: University of California Press, 1985), Part 2.
34 Dennis C. Mueller, *Public Choice II* (Cambridge, MA: Cambridge University Press, 1989), Chapter 5. Also see Anthony Downs, *An Economic Theory of Democracy* (New York: Harper Collins Publishers, 1957), Chapter 8. For an advanced text of spatial theory, see James M. Enelow and Melvin J. Hinich, eds, *Advances in the Spatial Theory of Voting* (Cambridge, MA: Cambridge University Press, 1990); for an elementary level of spatial theory, Melvin J. Hinich and Michael C. Munger, *Analytical Politics* (Cambridge, MA: Cambridge University Press, 1997); and for an intermediate level of spatial theory, Peter C. Ordeshook, *Game Theory and Political Theory: An Introduction* (Cambridge, MA: Cambridge University Press, 1986).
35 This idea originated from the 'Federalist Papers,' particularly, nos. 10 and 51.
36 Douglas W. Rae and Michael Taylor, *The Analysis of Political Cleavages* (New Haven, CT: Yale University Press, 1970), 106–8.
37 The underlying assumption is that transaction costs decrease when a cleavage structure and an issue agenda get simpler.
38 Malaysia is sometimes considered an instance of consociationalism. To avoid some misunderstanding on the part of those who are familiar with the literature on consociational democracy, I have to note that Arend Lijphart makes a distinction between consensual and majoritarian democracies. A prototype of his 'consensual' democracy is consociational democracy. However, consensual elites in elite theory can be observed in either majoritarian or 'consensual' democracy. In other words, 'consensual' democracy always has consensual elites, but consensual elites do not necessarily lead to 'consensual' democracy. To avoid any confusion over the term of consensus, it would be better to equate Lijphart's term of consensus with supermajority or unanimity rule. See Lijphart, *Democracies*.

2 The outbreak of the Asian economic crisis and its socioeconomic consequences

1 For other economic indicators, refer to Table 2.1 at the end of this chapter.
2 World Bank, *The East Asian Miracle: Economic Growth and Public Policy* (Oxford: Oxford University Press, 1993).
3 *Financial Times*, 12 January 1998, 6–7; 13 January 1998, 7–8; 14 January 1998, 6–7; 15 January 1998, 8; and 16 January 1998, 6 and 8.

4 'S Korean President Said Indonesia Crisis Due to Lack of Democracy,' *Agence France-Presse* (via *ClariNet*), 21 May 1998. Some scholars, however, view democracy as partially responsible for the economic crisis. For instance, Jongryn Mo and Chung-in Moon, 'Democracy and the Korean Economic Crisis,' paper presented to the Policy Forum Online of Northeast Asia Peace and Security Network, http://www.nautilus.org, 18 March 1998.

5 Stephan Haggard, *The Political Economy of the Asian Financial Crisis* (Washington, DC: Institute for International Economics, 2000), 10–11.

6 Among others, see Charles Wyplosz, 'Globalized Financial Markets and Financial Crisis,' paper prepared for presentation at the conference on 'Coping with Financial Crises in Developing and Transition Countries: Regulatory and Supervisory Challenges in a New Era of Global Finance' organized by the Forum on Debt and Development in Amsterdam, 16–17 March 1998; Warwick J. McKibbin, 'The Crisis in Asia: An Empirical Assessment,' manuscript, the Brookings Institution, 25 March 1998; and Steven Radelet and Jeffrey Sachs, 'The Onset of the East Asian Financial Crisis,' manuscript, Harvard Institute for International Development, 30 March 1998.

7 Charles Wolf, Jr., 'Too Much Government Control,' *Wall Street Journal,* 4 February 1998; and Giancarlo Corsetti, Paolo Pesenti, and Nouriel Roubini, 'What Caused the Asian Currency and Financial Crisis?' manuscript, March 1998.

8 Joseph Stiglitz, 'Bad Private-Sector Decisions,' *Wall Street Journal,* 4 February 1998. See also Wyplosz, 'Financial Crisis.'

9 Wolf Jr., 'Government Control.' Also see Corsetti, Pesenti, and Roubini, 'Financial Crisis' and Haggard, *The Asian Financial Crisis.*

10 For a comprehensive review of the decline of state-interventionism, Daniel Yergin and Joseph Stanislaw, *The Commanding Heights: The Battle between Government and the Marketplace that Is Remaking the Modern World* (New York: Simon & Schuster, 1998).

11 Paul Krugman, 'Asia: What Went Wrong?' *Fortune,* 2 March 1998; Louis Uchitelle, 'Economists Blame Short-Term Loans for Asian Crisis,' *New York Times on the Web,* 8 January 1998; and Corsetti, Pesenti, and Roubini, 'Financial Crisis.'

12 Even Haggard, who highlights the importance of domestic factors, admits, 'the catalog of [domestic] vulnerabilities outlined here does not, in itself, constitute a theory of financial crises but only a set of factors that can increase the propensity to crises and compound the costs *when they strike.*' Haggard, *The Asian Financial Crisis,* 46 (emphasis added).

13 'Hedge Funds Triggered Thai Financial Crisis: IMF,' *Agence France-Presse* (via *ClariNet*), 16 April 1998. The IMF study is in line with a *Financial Times* report saying that 'Asian Stock markets and currencies went into free fall in the last months of 1997. Hedge funds, on the other hand, surprisingly prospered.' 'The Long and the Short of It: Hedge Funds have Prospered amid the Asian Financial Crisis,' *Financial Times,* 12 January 1998, London edition, 21.

14 A Taiwan central bank survey shows that as of the end of March 1988, Japan had 223.6 billion dollars in its foreign exchange reserves; China, 140.6; Hong Kong, 96.8; and Taiwan, 83.6. *Digital Chosunilbo,* http://www.chosun.com (in Korean), 27 April 1998. For other reasons, see Steven Mufson, 'Outcome of Asian Economic Crisis Vital to China's Future,' *Washington Post,* 29 October 1997, A27.

15 Jungug Choi, 'Capital Flows, Political Cleavages and Economic Policy Choice: Malaysia during the Asian Economic Crisis,' *The Southeast Asian Review* 13 (Spring 2003): 383–400.

16 'The Philippines exited from 35 years of IMF stewardship of its economy last March [1998]. However, as a precaution against any resurgence of the Asian financial crisis, Manila agreed to an arrangement with the IMF committing itself to certain fiscal targets in exchange for a 1.37-billion-dollar standby IMF loan.' 'Philippines to Show

"Substantial Compliance" with IMF Review.' *Agence France-Presse* (via *ClariNet*), 14 May 1998.

17 Mitsuo Sato, Asian Development Bank President, is one of the few who made this point. Martin Abbugao, 'Asian Financial Crisis is Nearing its End: ADB Chief,' *Agence France-Presse,* 15 April 1998.

18 Steven Mufson, 'Outcome of Asian Economic Crisis Vital to China's Future,' *Washington Post,* 29 October 1997, A27. Also see an ADB statement, 'ADB to Loan Thailand US $ 500 MLN to Cushion Crisis Impact,' *Asia Pulse* (via *Lexis-Nexis*), 16 March 1998.

19 Chalongphob Sussangkarn, 'Thailand's Debt Crisis and Economic Outlook,' *Business Times* (Singapore), 31 January 1998.

20 Steven Pearlstein, 'Understanding the Asian Economic Crisis,' *Washington Post,* 18 January 1998, final edition, A32.

21 Hardev Kaur, 'Getting to the Bottom of the Asian Financial Crisis,' *Business Times* (Malaysia), 16 February 1998, 4. The comment was made by Jeffrey Sachs, Director of Harvard Institute for International Development. He continued to say, "history of capitalism is written by the creditors' who now allege that 'misguided, flawed and corrupt' governments are responsible for the private sector financial crisis in Asia.'

22 John Markoff and Silvio R. Duncan Baretta, 'Economic Crisis and Regime Change in Brazil: The 1960s and the 1980s,' *Comparative Politics* (July 1990): 436.

23 An outstanding exception to this was the case of the Long Term Capital Management, one of the prominent hedge funds, holding about 90 billions. The fund lost billions of dollars, especially in Russian financial markets. The US Federal Reserve Bank of New York intervened to rescue the failing fund by coordinating the 3.5 billion bailout plan in late September 1998. *New York Times* (via *Lexis-Nexis*), 25 September 1998.

24 World Bank, *East Asia: The Road to Recovery* (Washington, DC: The World Bank, 1998); Haggard, *The Asian Financial Crisis;* Asian Development Bank, *Asia Recovery Report 2000,* http://aric.adb.org, March 2000; T. J. Pempel, ed., *The Politics of the Asian Economic Crisis* (Ithaca, Cornell University Press, 1999); Organization for Economic Cooperation and Development, *OECD Economic Surveys: Korea 1998–1999* (in Korean) (Paris: OECD, 1999); Thailand Development Research Institute, *Social Impacts of the Asian Economic Crisis in Thailand, Indonesia, Malaysia, and the Philippines* (Bangkok: TDRI, 1999); K. S. Jomo , *Tigers in Trouble: Financial Governance, Liberalization and Crises in East Asia* (London: Zed Books, 1998); Manuel C. Difuntorum, 'The Political and Social Implications of the Asian Crisis,' *Kasarinlan: A Philippine Quarterly of Third Word Studies* 13, no. 4 (1998): 35–40; Jude Esguerra, 'The Impact of the Financial Crisis on Labor, Work, and Employment,' *Kasarinlan: A Philippine Quarterly of Third Word Studies* 13, no. 4 (1998): 67–78; Hyungpyo Moon, Hyehoon Lee, and Gyeongjoon Yoo, *Economic Crisis and Its Social Consequences* (Seoul: Korea Development Institute, 1999); Linda Y. C. Lim, Frank Ching, and Bernardo M. Villegas, *The Asian Economic Crisis: Policy Choices, Social Consequences, and the Philippine Case* (New York: Asia Society, 1999).

25 'Mahathir Warns of "Absolute Capitalism" as Emerging Ideology,' *Agence France-Presse* (via *ClariNet*), 28 May 1998.

26 For the early Malaysian policies coping with the crisis, see Ho Wah Foon, 'Malaysia Well Placed to Ride Out Financial Crisis,' *Straits Times* (Singapore), 14 November 1997, 82; and Anil Noel Netto, 'Malaysia: Asian Crisis Puts Brake on Rapid-Growth Strategy,' *Inter Press Service* (via *Lexis-Nexis*), 9 September 1997. For the final policy shifts, see the chapter of this volume about postcrisis Malaysia.

27 An exceptional scholarly complaint against the US dominance is Robert Wade and Frank Veneroso, 'The Asian Crisis: The High Debt Model vs. The Wall Street-Treasury-IMF Complex,' *New Left Review* 228 (March–April 1998): 3–22.

28 Nicholas D. Kristof, 'Crisis Pushing Asian Capitalism Closer to U.S. Style Free Market,' *New York Times on the Web*, 17 January 1998.
29 Kaur, 'Getting to the Bottom of the Asian Financial Crisis,' *Business Times* (Malaysia), 16 February 1998.
30 Stanley Fischer, 'The Asian Crisis: A View from the IMF,' address at the Midwinter Conference of Bankers' Association for Foreign Trade, 22 January 1998. This address is available at http://www.imf.org.
31 'Thai Central Bank Figures Show Economy Still in Decline,' *Agence France-Presse* (via *ClariNet*), 29 May 1998. For other postcrisis economic indicators, see Table 2.1.
32 Richard W. Baker, 'Indonesia in Crisis,' *Asia Pacific Issues: Analysis from the East-West Center* 36 (May 1998): 3. Also see 'FOCUS-Dark Days Lie Ahead for Asia's Workers,' *Reuters (*via *ClariNet), 29 April 1998.
33 'A Worsening Income Gap,' *Hankookilbo* (in Korean), 23 July 1998.
34 *Hankookilbo* (in Korean), 22 August 1998.
35 For instance, Haggard, *The Asian Financial Crisis*.
36 This was largely due to remittances from estimated 4 to 6 million overseas Filipino workers. They sent back 4.73 billion dollars in 1995, 7.5 in 1996, 5.7 in 1997, 4.93 in 1998, and 6.79 in 1999. *Dow Jones International News*, 11 September 1997 and 23 December 1998; *Associated Press Newswires*, 8 January 1997; and *Dow Jones Asian Equities Report*, 3 April 2000.

3   Political circumstances before the Asian economic crisis: Elite configurations in the five countries

1 John Higley and Michael Burton, 'Elite Transformation in Democratization's Three Waves,' paper delivered to the International Political Science Association World Congress, Quebec, August 2000.
2 Raj Vasil, *Governing Indonesia: National Development and Democracy* (Singapore: Butterworth-Heinemann Asia, 1997), 55.
3 'About 500,000 innocent communists, peasants, workers, schoolteachers, youth and women were mercilessly killed by the Army's crack troops, the RPKAD [Army Para-commandos], and fanatic Moslem youths incited by landowners, businessmen and anti-communist military like General Nasution and Sukendro. About 250,000 other innocent persons were arrested. Still the military [were] detaining without trial about 100,000 political prisoners in various prisons and concentration camps.' Ernst Utrecht, 'The Military Elite,' in *Ten Years' Military Terror in Indonesia*, ed. Malcolm Caldwell (Nottingham, England: the Bertrand Russell Peace Foundation for Spokesman Books, 1975), 14. As late as 1985 and 1986, a number of long-imprisoned [PKI] party leaders were executed.' Meanwhile, 'some 30,000 political detainees, including most of those held since the abortive 1965 coup, were freed under a government program that concluded in December 1979.' Arthur S. Banks, ed., *Political Handbook of the World: 1987* (Binghamton, NY: CSA Publications, 1987), 265–6.
4 Herbert Feith, *The Indonesian Elections of 1955* (Ithaca, NY: Department of Far Eastern Studies, Cornell University, 1957), 58–9.
5 Vasil, *Governing Indonesia*, 115. The two political parties as well as Golkar received financial aids from the Suharto government.
6 For history of Golkar, see David Reeve, *Golkar of Indonesia: An Alternative to the Party System* (Singapore: Oxford University Press, 1985).
7 For election results, see Jamie Mackie and Andrew MacIntyre, 'Politics,' in *Indonesia's New Order: The Dynamics of Socioeconomic Transformation*, ed. Hal Hill (St Leonards, Australia: Allen & Unwin, 1994), 12, and Komisi Pemilihan Umum (General Election Commission), *Pemilu Indonesia dalam Angka dan Fakta Tahun 1995–1999* (Indonesian Elections with Figures and Facts 1995–1999) (Jakarta: KPU,

2000). To count the effective number, I use the formula, $1/\Sigma p^2$, where p represents a proportion of votes for a political party. The vote distribution, which I used to calculate the effective number of parties, was not immaculate. Yet, the vote distribution was closer to the reality than the seat distribution, and it contains significant information about the system to the extent that the elections were not completely manipulated.

8　The Indonesian New Order did not allow for strong political opposition, while there were a significant number of powerful opposition forces under Marcos's New Society. In addition, Marcos's New Society was essentially predatory and did not seek the common good. It was economically devastating. In contrast, Suharto's New Order was not so predatory; it was an economically successful case. Of course, much data and information recently revealed the opposite side of the New Order. The new literature emphasizes cronyism, business-related corruption, and the first family's private business ventures. Nonetheless, these new facts are only a facet of the New Order. The existence of cronyism and corruption does not negate the fact that the New Order was economically successful. Reports of the economy under Marcos are found in Belinda A. Aquino, *Politics of Plunder: The Philippines under Marcos* (Quezon City: Great Books Trading, 1987) and James K. Boyce, *The Political Economy of Growth and Impoverishment in the Marcos Era* (Manila: Ateneo de Manila University Press, 1993). For the Suharto family's businesses, see *Financial Times*, 16 January 1998, 6.

9　The Yogyakarta Students' Communication Forum and its successor groups, the non-Muslim and noncommunist Indonesian Students' Action Front (FAMI), the Marxist oriented Student Solidarity for Democracy in Indonesia (SMID), and the Jakarta Communication Forum for Islamic Students (FKMIK) attracted public attention. For more detailed descriptions of these groups and other oppositions, see Anders Uhlin, *Indonesia and the 'The Wave of Democratization': The Indonesian Pro-democracy Movement in a Changing World* (Richmond (UK): Curzon, 1997), Chapter 5.

10　Salim Said, 'Suharto's Armed Forces: Building a Power Base in New Order Indonesia, 1966–1998,' *Asian Survey* 38 (June 1998): 537.

11　Harold Crouch, 'Military–Civilian Relations in Indonesia in the Late Soeharto Era,' in *The Military in Politics: Southeast Asian Experiences*, ed., Wolfgan S. Heinz, Werner Pfennig and Victor T. King (Hull: Center for Southeast Asian Studies, University of Hull, 1990), 94–6. A similar attitudinal difference was observed in David Jenkins, *Suharto and His Generals: Indonesian Military Politics 1975–1983* (Ithaca, NY: Cornell Modern Indonesia Project, Southeast Asia Program, Cornell University, 1984).

12　Said, 'Armed Forces,' 539. The original source is Benedict Anderson, Takashi Shiraishi, and James T. Siegel, eds., 'Current Data on the Indonesian Military Elite,' *Indonesia* 36 (October 1983): 111.

13　Before this event, 'the armed forces were always commanded either by Javanese officers from non-pious Muslim families or by officers from ethnic and/or religious minorities.' Said, 'Armed Forces,' 545.

14　Ibid., 545. For a slightly different presentation of the military factions, see *Asiaweek*, 20 February 1998, 25.

15　Benedict Anderson, Takashi Sharaishi, and James T. Siegel, eds., 'Current Data on the Indonesian Military Elite: October 1, 1995–December 31, 1997,' *Indonesia* 65 (April 1998): 184.

16　Hal Hill, 'The Economy,' in *Indonesia's New Order: The Dynamics of Socioeconomic Transformation*, ed. Hal Hill (St Leonards, Australia: Allen & Unvin, 1994), 54–5. Also see Hal Hill, *The Indonesian Economy since 1966: Southeast Asia's Emerging Giant* (New York: Cambridge University Press, 1996).

17　Duncan McCargo, *Chamlong Srimuang and the New Thai Politics* (London: Hurst & Company, 1997), 305.

18　All of the senators were nominated and supposed to be nonpartisan.

19　*Far Eastern Economic Review (FEER)*, 3 April 1981, 8–10; 1 May 1981, 12–3; 19 June 1981, 44; 18 September 1986, 44; 28 September 1989, 26; 1 August 1991, 20;

5 September 1991, 21; 29 September 1994, 16; 23 September 1993, 18; 21 September 1995, 19; 18 January 1996, 22; and 5 September 1996, 18. Also see some relevant entries of May Kyi Win and Harold E. Smith, *Historical Dictionary of Thailand* (London: The Scarecrow Press, Inc, 1995).
20 Barbara Leitch LePoer, ed., *Thailand: A Country Study* (Washington DC: Federal Research Division, Library of Congress, 1989), 208.
21 *FEER*, 7 March 1991, 18.
22 The first Chuan Leekpai government ran from 1992 to 1995.
23 *Economist*, 2 March 1991, 33.
24 *FEER,*18 December 1994. Arthit Kamlangek was appointed later as deputy prime minister as a member of the Chart Pattana party in the Cabinet led by Prime Minister Chuan Leekpai in December 1994. *Straits Times* (Singapore), 19 December 1994, 15.
25 *FEER*, 20 May 1993, 21.
26 Ibid., 23.
27 Renato S. Velasco, 'Philippine Democracy: Promise and Performance,' in *Democratization in Southeast and East Asia*, ed. Anek Laothamatas (New York: St Martin's Press, 1997), 83.
28 For land reform issues, see Jeffrey M. Riedinger, *Agrarian Reform in the Philippines: Democratic Transitions and Redistributive Reform* (Stanford, CA: Stanford University Press, 1995) and James Putzel, *A Captive Land: the Politics of Agrarian Reform in the Philippines* (London: CIIR, 1992).
29 Michael Leifer, *Dictionary of the Modern Politics of South-East Asia* (London: Routledge, 1995), 47–8.
30 Ibid., 154–5.
31 Carl H. Lande, *Post Marcos Politics: A Geographical and Statistical Analysis of the 1992 Presidential Election* (New York: St Martin's Press, 1996), 52.
32 Velasco, 'Philippine Democracy,' 101. For details, see Eric Gutierrez, *The Ties that Bind* (Makati: Philippine Center for Investigative Journalism, 1994).
33 Article 6. 5. (2) of the 1987 constitution. The whole text is available in Martin Wright, ed., *Revolution in the Philippines?: A Keesing's Special Reports* (Chicago, IL: St. James Press, 1988).
34 Yoshihara Kunio, *Philippine Industrialization: Foreign and Domestic Capital* (Quezon City: Ateneo de Manila University Press, 1985), Chapters 5 and 6. Paul D. Hutchcroft, 'Predatory Oligarchy, Patrimonial State: The Politics of Banking in the Philippines,' in *Pattern of Power and Politics in the Philippines: Implications for Development*, ed., James F. Eder and Robert L. Youngblood (Tempe, AZ: Arizona State University, 1994).
35 *Philippine Daily Inquirer*, 17 June 1992. These official results are available at the Social Weather Stations official website, http: // www.sws.org.ph/statcon2.htm. Also see Lande, *Post-Marcos Politics*, Chapter 2.
36 Richard J. Kessler, *Rebellion and Repression in the Philippines* (New Haven: Yale University Press, 1989), 57. For a different estimate of the communist strength, see Joe V. Abueva, Maria Serena I. Diokno, R. B. Rodil, Abrino Aydinan, and Temario C. Rivera, *Ending the Armed Conflicts: Peace Negotiations in the Philippines* (Diliman, Quezon City: University of the Philippines Press, 1992), 11.
37 'Influence' means that 50 percent of the residents were sympathetic.
38 Arthur S. Banks, *Political Handbook of the World: 1998* (Binghamton, NY: CSA Pub lications, 1998), 671.
39 Ibid., 671.
40 For details about the peace negotiations, see Fidel V. Ramos, *Break Not the Peace: The Story of the GRP-MNLF Peace Negotiations 1992–1996* (Quezon City: The Friends of Steady Eddie, 1996).
41 Banks, *Political Handbook*, 671.
42 Velasco, 'Philippine Democracy,' 93–4.

43 Gretchen Casper, *Fragile Democracies: The Legacies of Authoritarian Rule* (Pittsburgh, PA: University of Pittsburgh Press, 1995), 136.

44 For details of the coups, see ibid., 141–4 and 167–9. And also see Mark R. Thompson, *The Anti-Marcos Struggle: Personalistic Rule and Democratic Transition in the Philippines* (New Haven: Yale University Press, 1995),168–0. Despite these continuing failures, it should be noted that politically oriented military officers, mostly younger, 'believe that "regardless of the constitution, the armed forces have the right to intervene in politics, especially in the reestablishment of civilian institutions."' Casper, *Fragile Democracies*, 148. This overall attitude of younger officers is also confirmed in Thompson, *Anti-Marcos Struggle*, 133–4. 'A poll of five hundred officers conducted in April-May 1987 indicated this changed viewpoint: 96 percent believed the military should play a role in national development; 61 percent thought that officers were as capable as civilian officials in civilian positions; 50 percent wanted more military men in public office. . . .'

45 Abdul Rashid Moten and Tunku Mohar Mokhtar, 'The 1995 General Elections in Malaysia: A Trend Analysis,' *Asian Profile* 25 (February 1997): 41–2.

46 Other possible origins of the Malay Alliance are listed in Donald L. Horowitz, *Ethnic Groups in Conflict* (Berkeley: University of California Press, 1985), 402–3.

47 Kiran Kapur Datar, *Malaysia: Quest for a Politics of Consensus* (New Delhi: Vikas Publishing House PVT Ltd, 1983), 3.

48 Ibid., 4. Also see Alasdair Bowie and Danny Unger, *The Politics of Open Economies* (Cambridge, MA: Cambridge University Press, 1997), 59 and notes 5 and 6. There is a different viewpoint about the role of British colonial policy: 'It should be noted that this segregation did not represent any divide-and-rule policy on the part of the British, as it antedated the British arrival, but it was endemic to the whole region and beyond, even before the days of the Malacaa Sultanate. It was simply that the different racial groups preferred to live in their own areas, where they could feel at ease among their own people, and where they would not encounter problems on account of language, food, customs and religion.' See Leon Comber, *13 May 1969: A Historical Survey of Sino-Malay Relations* (Kuala Lumpur: Heinemann Asia, 1983).

49 The 1969 riots erupted against the background of the threatening increase in political influence of anti-Alliance political groups. Even though the Alliance maintained its majority seats in parliament in the 1969 elections, its opponents won more than 50 percent of the votes. Most notably, anti-Alliance Chinese political parties such as Democratic Action Party and Gerakan Ra'ayat Malaysia made a big progress. After the riots, the political and economic influence of the ethnic Chinese decreased. For the riots and its subsequent political reformulation such as the replacement of the Alliance with the National Front and the joining of some anti-Alliance parties to the former Alliance coalition, see Datar, *Malaysia*, Chapter 4; Felix V. Gagliano, 'Communal Violence in Malaysia 1969: The Political Aftermath,' papers in International Studies of Center for International Studies, Southeast Asia Series, no. 13. (Athens, GA: Ohio University, 1970); Comber, *13 May 1969*; N. J. Funston, *Malay Politics in Malaysia: A Study of the United Malays National Organization and Party Islam* (Kuala Lumpur: Heinemann Educational Books (Asia) Ltd., 1980), Chapter 9.

50 The estimated numbers of ethnic Chinese in Southeast Asia in 1990, with their percentage in each country being in parentheses, are as follows: Brunei 40,621 (16 percent); Burma 466,000 (1.4); Cambodia 50,000 (1.0); Indonesia 5,460,000 (3.0); Laos 10,000 (0.4); Malaysia 5,261,000 (29.6); Philippines 850,000 (1.3); Singapore 2,252,700 (77.7); Thailand 4,813,000 (8.6); Vietnam 962,000 (1.5); Total 20,165,321 (4.69). Some numbers here are for 1985. Leo Suryadinata, 'Ethnic Chinese in Southeast Asia: Overseas Chinese, Chinese Overseas or Southeast Asians?' in *Ethnic Chinese as Southeast Asians*, ed. Leo Suryadinata (New York: St Martin's Press, 1997), 21. For a discussion of why the Chinese became successful in business, see Robert Cribb, 'Political Structures and Chinese Business Connections in the Malay

World: A Historical Perspective,' in *Chinese Business Networks: State, Economy, and Culture*, ed. Chan Kwok Bun (Singapore: Prentice Hall, 2000).

51 The data come from the file of Facts and Figures in Malaysia's Country Profile of *Lexis-Nexis*.

52 By this I refer to a series of political skirmishes from 1987 to 1996: the intra-UMNO struggle between Team A represented by Mahathir and incumbent leaders and Team B led by Tengku Razaleigh and Musa Hitam, the nominal change of UMNO to UMNO Baru, Team B's ultimate defection from UMNO and regrouping in the name of Semangat 46 (Spirit of 1946), the dissolution of Semangat 46 and its reintegration into UMNO. See Khoo Boo Teik, *Paradoxes of Mahathirism: An Intellectual Biography of Mahathir Mohamad* (Kuala Lumpur: Oxford University Press, 1995), Chapters 6 and 7; Gordon P. Means, *Malaysian Politics: The Second Generation* (Singapore: Oxford University Press, 1991), Chapters 7 and 8.

53 Samuel P. Huntington, *The Third Wave: Democratization in the Late Twentieth Century* (Norman, OK: University of Oklahoma Press), 151–63; Michael Burton and Jai P. Ryu, 'South Korea's Elite Settlement and Democratic Consolidation,' *Journal of Political and Military Sociology* 25 (Summer 1997): 1–24. Also see Michael Burton and John Higley, 'Political Crises and Elite Settlements,' in *Elites, Crises, and the Origins of Regimes*, ed., Mattei Dogan and John Higley (Lanham, MD: Rowman & Littlefield Publishers, Inc., 1998).

54 The military or authoritarian regime in South Korea remained comparatively popular. The repression by the military regime was not pervasive and thorough in Korea compared to some Latin American countries, in part, due to its economic success and the military confrontation with North Korea. This is one of the reasons that the military and civilian camps disappeared so quickly and became virtually invisible by the mid-1990s. An exceptional event to this tendency was the so called 'Kwangju Incident,' or the violent crackdown of a democratic movement in Kwangju, one of the southern cities.

55 *Facts on File World News Digest*, 18 December 1987, 925.

56 Heemin Kim, 'Rational Choice Theory and Third World Politics: The 1990 Party Merger in Korea,' *Comparative Politics* 30 (October 1997): 83–100.

57 The poor performance of the governing party was also partly due to the fact that Chung Ju Young, the founder of Hyundai, formed a new party to contest President Roh's poor economic management. Chung's party obtained 17.4 percent of the vote or 10.1 percent of parliamentary seats. His party was dissolved after his defeat in the 1992 presidential election, facing Kim Young Sam's threats to retaliate. Consequently, the party failed to create a durable political cleavage that would replace or crosscut the regional or anti-democratic/democratic cleavages.

58 Chung Ju Young won 16.3, Park Chan Jong, 6.1, Paik Kee Wan, 1, and other two candidates, 0.2 and 0.4 respectively. *BBC Summary of World Broadcasts* (via *Lexis-Nexis*), 24 December 1992.

59 In an interview with a magazine editor, Kim Young Sam said that a government survey before the 1997 presidential election had shown that the Cholla population accounted for 27 percent of the total population and the Kyongsang population, for 39 percent. Daesuk Sung and Jaeyoung Choi, 'A Special Interview with Former President Kim Young Sam,' *The Monthly Politic and Economic News* (in Korean), August 2000, 44. These figures seem a bit high. The Korean government does not publish the population distribution according to their places of birth. Yet, random surveys show that the two regions jointly account for more than 50 percent of the total population and less than 70 percent, but most likely, around 60 percent.

60 This is a survey result, Institute for Korean Election Studies, *The 14th Korean Presidential Election Study* (in Korean), codebook (Seoul, 1993). Its sample size was 1200. The polling period was a week from one day after the election.

61 For policy volatility and gridlocks, Jongryn Mo, 'Political Learning and Democratic Consolidation: Korean Industrial Relations, 1987-1992,' *Comparative Political Studies* 29 (June 1996): 290–311, and 'Political Culture and Legislative Gridlock: Politics of Economic Reform in Pre-Crisis Korea,' manuscript, Yonsei University, January 2000. Mo explains the gridlock or policy failure with political culture. I contend, however, that regional political cleavages were responsible for those policy failures.

62 Inhak Hwang, *The Myths and Facts of the Korean Economic Concentration: The Comparative Analysis of Aggregate Concentration* (in Korean) (Seoul: Korean Economic Research Institute, 1997), 127–36.

63 Stephan Haggard, *The Political Economy of the Asian Financial Crisis* (Washington, D.C.: Institute for International Economics, 2000), 21–3.

64 A byproduct of the chaebol system was militant labor. Labor militancy was led by those workers that belonged to chaebols. Yet, despite their high visibility, their numerical strength remained small. The top 30 largest business groups employed only 873,159 out of the total 21,048,000 part-time and full-time employees, that is, 4.15 percent in 1997.

4 Economic crisis, divided elites, and prospects for an elite settlement

1 Nocola Bullard *et al.*, 'Taming the Tigers: The IMF and the Asian Crisis,' in *Tigers in Trouble: Financial Governance, Liberalization and Crises in East Asia*, ed. K. S. Jomo (Hong Kong: Hong Kong University Press, 1998), 94.

2 Michael Malley, 'The 7th Development Cabinet: Loyal to a Fault?' *Indonesia* 65 (April 1998): 156.

3 *Business Times* (Singapore), 21 March 1998.

4 *Jakarta Post,* http://www.thejakratapost.com, 9 April 1998.

5 Economist Intelligence Unit, *EIU Country Report: Indonesia,* second quarter 1998, 30.

6 A comprehensive list of protests and riots in 1998 and 1999 is found in 'Landscape of Potential for Unrest,' manuscript, Suara 234 (Voice of 234), Trisakti University's Research Center and Research Institute for Democracy and Peace (RIDeP), 6 May 1999.

7 For a succinct report of the US–Suharto relationship, see Noam Chomsky, 'Indonesia, Master Card in Washington's Hand,' *Indonesia* 66 (October 1998): 1–4. Notable figures that requested Suharto's resignation were Amien Rais, former ICMI board member, Harmoko, Speaker of both the upper and lower houses, and Ginandjar Kartasasmita, leader of a group of cabinet members.

8 For a different explanation of Suharto's resignation focusing primarily on domestic factors, see Adam Schwarz, *A Nation in Waiting: Indonesia's Search for Stability,* 2nd ed. (St Leonards, Australia: Allen & Unwin, 1999).

9 *Kompas,* http://www.kompas.com, 11 November 1998.

10 For the various responses to the Agreement, *Kompas,* 12 November 1998.

11 *Kompas,* 13 November 1998.

12 There were five factions in the MPR: an ABRI military Faction (FABRI, 113 members), a Development Work Faction including Golkar (FKP, 588), a Regional Representative Faction (FUD, 149), the nationalistic Indonesian Democratic Party (FPDI,16), and the Islamic United Development Party (KPP,134). *Kompas,* 14 November 1998 and MPR web sites, http://www.mpr.go.id/anggota/komposisi.htm and http://www.mpr.go.id/indexanggota.htm.

13 Later, in April 1999, the ABRI (Angkatan Bersenjata Republik Indonesia) was renamed TNI (Tentara Nasional Indonesia), while the national police force was separated from the military.

14 *Kompas,* 7 January 1999.
15 According to the MPR decree, no. VI/MPR/1999, on rules on presidential elections, a faction or any group of at least 70 MPR members can nominate a candidate. The candidacy should be submitted to the MPR leadership at least 12 hours before the vote. The election must be attended by at least two-thirds (if impossible, one-half) of the 700-members. Given that there are only three candidates, if no person wins an absolute majority in the first round, the top two candidates will go to the second round, where still absolute majority rule applies. If neither of the two candidates wins an absolute majority in the second and third rounds, alternative candidates must be proposed and will start again from the beginning.
16 We need to assume additionally that immediate reelection is not barred. Plurality rule by itself does not help to reduce the number of viable parties when a single-term limit system is adopted. Jungug Choi, 'Philippine Democracies Old and New: Elections, Term Limits, and Party Systems,' *Asian Survey* 41(May/June 2001): 488–501.
17 'The Republic of Indonesia Law Number 3 Year 1999 on General Election' in National Election Commission, *Collection of Electoral Laws* (Jakarta, 1999). About 30 of these 48 parties were formed between May and August in 1998.
18 Eleven percent of the popular vote for the others includes 9.17 percent of the national vote for the 27 parties that secured no seat. For the official election outcomes, see Komisi Pemilihan Umum (General Election Commission), *Pemilu Indonesia dalam Angka and Fakta Tahun 1995–1999* (Indonesian Elections with Figures and Facts 1995–1999) (Jakarta: KPU, 2000), 192.
19 On 17 May 1998, the three main opposition parties reaffirmed their alliance against Golkar. However, they did not actually coordinate their election campaigns.
20 In particular, Golkar was not exclusively secular even though it was not a clearly Muslim-based party. I also exclude PBB from my analysis since it was too small.
21 Jose Manuel Tesoro, 'Islam Has Been a Social and Spiritual Force. Now It Is Helping Reshaping Politics Too,' *Asiaweek,* 19 June 1998. For diverging views by the three major Muslim organizations on current Muslim issues, go to http://www.pathfinder.com/asiaweek/99/0129/nat2.html.
22 According to the MPR decree, no. II/MPR/1999, on rules of the MPR procedure, a faction or 'Fraksi' is 'a grouping of members that reflects the configuration of general election winning's political parties, Armed Forces/Police, and [Social] Group Delegates.' Notably, the factions were no longer required to vote in bloc. Thus, any decision by faction leadership was not to bind on its members.
23 Reformasi comprised PAN and the Justice Party. KKI was a group of eight small non-Muslim parties including the Justice and Unity Party (PKP) and the Indonesian Democratic Party (PDI). PDU was a group of five small Islamic parties that had participated in the eight-party stembus accoord excluding PPP, the Justice Party and the Crescent Star Party (PBB). PDKB is a single party faction of Love the Nation Democratic Party (PDKB). For more details, see MPR, *MRR Buku Kerja 2000 (MPR Workbook 2000)* (Jakarta: MPR, 2000) and National Election Commission, *DPR-MPR Member Profiles, 1999–2004* (in Indonesian) (Jakarta: NEC, 1999). Five regional representatives from East Timor were left vacant.
24 According to an MPR minute, the detailed results of MPR chairperson election were as follows: 2 votes for Husnie Thamrin (PPP), 4 for Nazri Adlani (UG), 279 for Matori Abdul Djalil (PKB), 10 for Ginandjar Kartasasmita (Golkar), 305 for Amien Rais (Reformasi), 5 for Kwik Kian Gie (PDI-P), 41 for Hari Sabarno (TNI/Polri), 1 for Jusuf Amir Feisal (PBB), with 3 abstentions. The minor candidates joined the race only to be elected vice chairperson. According to the MPR rules, 'the chairman's candidates who are not elected as Assembly's Chairmen[*sic*] shall be determined as Assembly's Vice Chairmen.'
25 For details, refer to note 15 in Chapter 4.

26 *Kompas*, 21 October 1999.
27 *Jakarta Post*, 2 October 1999.
28 *Jakarta Post*, 20 October 1999.
29 *jakarta Post*, 22 October 1999. Wiranto was nominated for the vice presidency by the PDU faction.
30 PDI-P or, more precisely, Megawati relied on her biggest but less-than-majority popular vote (about 34 percent) to claim the presidency while holding off from negotiations with other political elite groups. Megawati said, 'Our 35 percent [*sic*] is real. The other 65 percent is not.' This belief that 'the party won the general election, and therefore Megawati deserve[d] the presidential seat' was unacceptable to other elite groups and looked arrogant. *Jakarta Post*, 19–20 October 1999.
31 *EIU Country Report: Indonesia*, 4th quarter 1999, 15.

5 Economic crisis, fragmented elites, and prospects for elite convergence

1 Barbara Leitch LePoer, ed., *Thailand: A Country Study*, 6th edition (Washington, DC: Federal Research Division, Library of Congress, 1989), 149.
2 *Straits Times* (Singapore), 23 March 1996, 21.
3 LePoer, *Thailand*.
4 *Far Eastern Economic Review FEER*, 12 November 1998.
5 In 1988, Harn became party advisor of the new Prachachon or People party; yet, he, along with other eight followers teamed up with the Chart Thai party in 1989 instead of joining a newly merging Ekkaparb or Solidarity party as initially motioned by himself. *FEER*, 4 May 1989.
6 Devilish parties, meaning pro-military-junta parties, were opposed to angelic parties.
7 For a historical explanation of Thai communism, see John L. S. Girling, *Thailand: Society and Politics* (Ithaca, NY: Cornell University Press, 1981), Chapter 7. For some other reasons for weak communism in Thailand, see Yoshihara Kunio, *The Nation and Economic Growth: The Philippines and Thailand* (Kuala Lumpur: Oxford University Press, 1994), Chapter 12.
8 Concerning economic dominance by Chinese families, see an article titled 'Empires in the East; a Booming Economy in Thailand Has not Reduced the Domination of the Country's Powerful Chinese Families,' *Economist*, 26 January 1991, 64.
9 Kenneth Perry Landon, *The Chinese in Thailand* (New York, Russell & Russell, 1941), 16–17. For a more recent study of ethnic Chinese in Thai politics, see Curtis N. Thomson, 'Electoral Geography of the Sino-Thai in Thailand's National Elections, 1979–1995,' *Professional Geographer* 48 (November 1996): 392–404. This study, on page 402, concludes that 'Thailand is one of the few countries in Southeast Asia to assimilate the minority Chinese into their mainstream political system.'
10 Chai-Anan Samudavanija, 'Thailand: A Stable Semi-democracy,' in *Politics in Developing Countries: Comparing Experiences with Democracy*, ed., Larry Dimond, Juan J. Linz, and Seymour Martin Lipset, 2nd ed. (Boulder, MA: Lynne Rienner Publishers, 1995), 347.
11 Mark R. Thompson, *The Anti-Marcos Struggle: Personalistic Rule and Democratic Transition in the Philippines* (New Haven: Yale University Press, 1995), 6.
12 Kunio, *The Nation and Economic Growth*, 37.
13 Negative legacies of Spanish and American rule in the relations between the ethnic Chinese and the native Filipinos are not completely absent, as seen in Teresita Ang See, 'The Ethnic Chinese as Filipinos,' in *Ethnic Chinese as Southeast Asians*, ed. Leo

Suryadinata (New York: St Martin's Press, 1997), 168–9. Nonetheless, they remain comparatively weak.

14   Kunio, *The Nation and Economic Growth*, 181–2.
15   Carl Lande, *Post-Marcos Politics: A Geographical and Statistical Analysis of the 1992 Presidential Election* (New York: St. Martin's Press, 1996), 60.
16   Ibid., 81.
17   Ledivina V. Carino, 'The Land and the People,' in *Government and Politics of the Philippines*, ed. Raul P. de Guzman and Mila A. Reforma (New York: Oxford University Press, 1988) 10. For a through description of etho-linguistic groups, go to a website, http://www.sil.org/ethologue.
18   Karl W. Deutsch, 'Social Mobilization and Political Development,' *American Political Science Review* 53 (September 1961): 493–514.
19   *Agence France-Presse* (via *ClariNet*), 4 May 1998.
20   *Financial Times*, 16 July 1997.
21   *Los Angles Times*, 15 July 1997.
22   *Agence Fance-Presse* (via *ClariNet*), 4 May 1998.
23   This was one of the reasons that, as noted later, many representatives voted, albeit hesitantly, for a reform constitution, which would allow them to hang on for additional 240 days.
24   *Bangkok Post*, 6 August 1997. For other conflicts between the Chart Pattana and other government ministers, see Andrew MacIntyre, 'Political Institutions and the Economic Crisis in Thailand and Indonesia,' in *The Politics of the Asian Economic Crisis*, ed. T. J. Tempel (Ithaca, NY: Cornell University Press, 1999), 149–53.
25   *FEER*, 18 September 1997, 16.
26   For a full English text of the new constitution, refer to the Thai Parliament website, http://www.parliament.go.th. For an analysis of the process of constitutional revision, see Prudhisan Jumbala, 'Thailand: Constitutional Reform amidst Economic Crisis,' in *Southeast Asian Affairs 1998* (Singapore: Institute of Southeast Asian Studies, 1998), 265–91 and Suchit Bunbongkarn, 'Thailand's Successful Reforms,' *Journal of Democracy* 10 (October 1999): 54–68.
27   *FEER*, 18 September 1997, 14–16; *FEER*, 9 October 1997, 16 and 20.
28   These three bills were passed by 29 May 1998. However, calls for early elections after the passage were dismissed by then Prime Minister Chuan Leekpai, who said that he would not call for elections until the economic crisis was over. *Agence France-Presse* (via *ClariNet*), 29 May 1998.
29   *FEER*, 6 November 1997, 20.
30   *Bangkok Post*, 5 September 1997 and *FEER*, 6 September 1997, 21. The overall political attitudes of the Thai military were reviewed in an article of *FEER*, 29 January 1998, 22–3.
31   *FEER*, 20 November 1997, 28.
32   *Nation*, 19 November 1996.
33   *Asiaweek*, 7 November 1997, 20–1.
34   *FEER*, 13 November 1997, 14–15. Also, *Asiaweek*, 14 November 1997, 22–3.
35   For the defection, see *Bangkok Post*, 10 November 1997. For key events in the horse-trading, see *Bangkok Post*, 8 November 1997, 1.
36   Meanwhile, Chavalit's outgoing coalition was made up of his New Aspiration (125), Chat Pattana (52), Social Action (20), Prachakorn Thai (18), Seritham (4), and Muanchon (2).
37   *FEER*, 15 October 1998, 21. At this time, the party was led by Korn Dabbaransi, cousin of the former leader, Chatichai, who died of liver cancer in May 1998. The opposition leader, Chavalit, often called on Chuan to resign, but his demand was not serious since he disagreed with the dissolution of parliament, saying 'if the prime minister doesn't want to resign, he should not resort to a House dissolution.' *Bangkok Post*, 1 January 1999.

38 Segundo E. Romero, 'The Philippines in 1997: Weathering Political and Economic Turmoil,' *Asian Survey* 38 (February 1998): 196–202.

39 *Asiaweek*, 3 October 1997.

40 The word, chacha, was coined by opposition Congressman John Osmena. *South China Morning Post* (via *Lexis-Nexis*), 1 September 1997, 10.

41 *Business World* (Manila, via *Dow Jones Interactive*), 28 August 1997.

42 *Straits Times* (Singapore, via *Lexis-Nexis*), 7 September 1997, 25.

43 *Asiaweek*, 3 October 1997. Although prospective presidential candidates including Estrada and Senator Gloria Macapagal Arroyo were on the grandstand, they did not play the leading role.

44 The constitutional amendment issue resurfaced with regard to the nomination of the governing Lakas-NUCD party's presidential candidate. According to a report, Ramos anointed Speaker Jose de Venecia as the party's standard bearer partly because de Venecia, a known advocate of parliamentary system, proposed to make Ramos prime minister through a post-election constitutional change. On the other hand, former Defense Secretary Renato de Villa had openly opposed the plans to change the constitution during the debates in September 1997. *Business Daily* (via *Dow Jones Interactive*), 5 January 1998.

45 In the May elections, each voter votes for ten senators, one party-list representative, congressional representative, governor, five provincial board members, city mayor and vice major, and ten city council members in addition to president and vice president at the same time. In the May elections, a total of 83,811 candidates ran. Ten of them ran for presidency, 9 for vice presidency, 40 for senate, 853 for congress, 331 for governor, 296 for vice governor, 2,334 for provincial board members, and the rest for municipal/city mayor, vice mayor, and councilor. *Philippine Headline News Online*, http://www.newsflash.org, 10 July 1998.

46 *The Social Weather Stations*, http://www.sws.org.ph/exit-com.htm#pres.

47 *Xinhua News Agency* (via *Lexis-Nexis*), 11 June 1997.

48 *Business World* (Manila, via *Lexis-Nexis*), 17 October 1997.

49 Crime and women's rights were middle or upper class issues, while regional development overlapped the issue of poverty. Afredo Lim was Liberal Party candidate, a Filipino Chinese and former police general, his candidacy being endorsed by the Catholic Church and Corazon Aquino. He was known as 'Dirty Harry' because he 'put Manila's red light district out of business when he became mayor in 1992, during which the tattooed corpses of suspected gangsters began to regularly float on the city's open sewers.' Raul Roco was born to wealthy landowners, and his power basis lay in the eastern region of Bicol. He was Aksyon Demokratiko or Democratic Action Party candidate and senator who earned the title of 'honorary woman' because he advanced women's causes. However, he also 'helped draft and endorse a since defunct 1971 constitution which critics say legitimized the Ferdinand Marcos dictatorship.' *Agence France-Presse* (via *Clarinet*), 5 May 1998. For the profiles of presidential candidates, go to http://www.webweaver.com.ph/presidentiables.

50 *Agence France-Presse* (via *ClariNet*), 7 May 1998.

51 Ibid.

52 This is defined as proportion of families whose annual per capita income falls below the annual per capita poverty threshold, out of the total number of families.

53 The sources were the website of National Statistical Coordination Board, http://www.nscb.gov.ph, and its subdirectory, http://www.nscb.gov.ph/poverty/97povin.htm.

54 The results of the survey were posted at a Social Weather Stations website, http://www.sws.org.ph/exitpsdc.htm. Yet, the same survey showed that there was no much difference in voting for de Venecia across the classes. Rather, strangely enough, it showed that more respondents in the upper class had voted for Lim (19.5%) or for Roco (26%) than for de Venecia (12.6%). However, more middle-class respondents voted for de Venecia (16.6%) than for Roco (13.4%) or Lim (9.2%).

55 *Philippine Headline News Online,* http://www.newsflash.org, 14 July 1998.
56 *Asiaweek,* 9 October 1998.
57 *Asiaweek,* 8 May 1998.
58 Roco secured about 70 percent votes in Region V or Bicol, which was higher than any support rate for any single candidate in any other region in the Philippines, according to the above-mentioned Social Weather Stations exit poll.
59 *Philippine Headline News Online,* 6 July 1998. However, Cebu Representative Eduardo Gullas filed a bill, House Bill No. 86, 'prohibiting senators from continuing their unfinished terms after losing in either presidential or vice presidential elections.'
60 Jungug Choi, 'Philippine Democracies Old and New: Elections, Term Limits and Party System.' *Asian Survey* 41 (May/June 2001): 497–9.
61 I do not deal with the other anti-system force, Muslim separatists. This is due not only to the limited space available to me but also to a theoretical presumption that ethnic political cleavages are not conducive to elite convergence, as noted in Chapter 1.
62 *Business World,* 5 January 1998. The National Democratic Front of the Philippines is the negotiation arm of the Communist Party. It seeks, among others, (1) to overthrow the semi-colonial and semi-feudal system through a people's war, (2) to establish a people's democratic republic, (3) to build the people's army, (4) to implement genuine agrarian reform, and (5) to break the United States-big comprador-landlord dominance over the economy. *Business World,* 10 March 1999.
63 *Business World,* 4 February 1998, 16–17 March 1998.
64 *Business World,* 20 March 1998.
65 Only in August 1998, did the principals of the government and the NDFP approve the agreement. Their approval was required for it to be effective and binding.
66 *Business World,* 8 October 1998.
67 Ibid.
68 *Business World,* 25 February 1999 and 10 March 1999.
69 *Business World,* 27 April 1999.
70 *Business World,* 30 April 1999.
71 *Business World,* 5 May 1999.
72 'The VFA is the operational pact that would allow joint military exercises and would give teeth to how the Philippines-United States Mutual Defense Treaty would be operational in case of an actual foreign aggression into Philippines sovereignty.' *Business World,* 22 April 1999.
73 *Business World,* 22 April 1999.
74 *Business World,* 2 February 1999.
75 *FEER,* 17 June 1999.

6 Economic crisis, consensual elites, and prospects for the further consensus

1 Cross-voters are here defined as those who abandon their traditional party affiliation and then discretely either vote for another party or abstain from voting.
2 Richard Leete, *Malaysia's Demographic Transition: Rapid Development, Culture, and Politics* (Kuala Lumpur: Oxford University Press, 1996), 185. According to the same source, the detailed projection over years is as follows:

	Bumiputera	Chinese	Indians	Total
1991	61.4	28.4	7.9	100.0
2001	64.7	25.7	7.3	100.0
2011	67.8	23.3	6.8	100.0
2021	70.3	21.3	6.4	100.0

3 Edmund Terence Gomez and K. S. Jomo, *Malaysia's Political Economy: Politics, Patronage and Profits* (Cambridge, MA: Cambridge University Press, 1997), 168. There are some other categories of ownership so that the sum of the three does not make 100 percent. A revised version of this book was published in 1999, with a new chapter on the crisis, 'Afterword: From Economic to Political Crisis.'

4 For a summary of this policy package, see Samuel Bassey Okposin and Cheng Ming Yu, *Economic Crises in Malaysia: Causes, Implications, and Policy Prescriptions* (Selangor Darul Ehsan, Malaysia: Pelanduk Publications, 2000), Appendix 8.

5 *Utusan Express* at http://www.utusan.com.my/, 30 August 1998.

6 *Far Eastern Economic Review* (*FEER*) at http://www.feer.com/, 24 June 1999.

7 However, 'The rule on one-year holding of portfolio capital was liberalized from February 15 this year [1999] to allow foreign investors to repatriate principal capital and profits, subject to a graduated levy depending upon when the funds were brought into Malaysia and the duration of the investment.' *Utusan Express*, 1 September 1999.

8 *Utusan Express*, 4 September 1999. As early as 12 August, 1998, Daim informed Anwar that he would be charged in court, and he threatened Anwar to resign. *Utusan Express*, 23 October 1999.

9 *Utusan Express*, 29 September 1998.

10 This raised speculation that Anwar was hoping to rejoin UMNO in a post-Mahathir period. However, Keadilan announced, in September 1999, that he joined the party as an ordinary member as well as advisor to the party. This was one day after his nomination as Alternative Front (BA) candidate for Prime Minister. His membership was approved on September 15. *Deutsche Presse-Agentur* (via *Lexis-Nexis*), 22 September 1999.

11 *Utusan Express*, August 1, 1999. The Agenda for Change also included some economic issues, such as introduction of a minimum living wage, review of the policy and practice of privatization, and initiation of an open tender policy in the award of contracts and privatization projects. It was additionally committed to Islam as a way of life among the Muslims and to the right of non-Muslims to practice their own religions in peace and harmony.

12 Hari Singh, 'Democratization or Oligarchic Restructuring? The Politics of Reform in Malaysia,' *Government and Opposition*, 35 (autumn 2000): 520–46.

13 This name came from *FEER*, 5 August 1999, 18.

14 In August 1999, three opposition parties in Sarawak – Keadilan, Sarawak State Reformation Party (STAR), and DAP – also formed a coalition called the Sarawak Alternative Front, to contest all the 27 parliamentary seats against BN in the coming election. They, however, agreed not to use a common symbol. *Utusan Express*, 16 August 1999.

15 *Utusan Express*, 21 June 1999.

16 *Utusan Express*, 26 June 1999.

17 According to the Federal Constitution, a person is disqualified as an MP if she or he is jailed for a year or fined RM 2000. In April 1999, Anwar was sentenced to six years in jail for four counts of corrupt practice of interfering in police investigations into allegations of his sexual misconduct. *Utusan Express*, 15 April 1999.

18 After Anwar's lawyer claimed that he suffered from arsenic poisoning, based on tests on his urine samples done secretly in an Australian laboratory, he was admitted to hospital on September 10. Later, a report by a Malaysian medical team revealed that he did not suffer from acute or chronic arsenic poisoning. *Utusan Express*, 5 October 1999.

19 However, a new budget would have to be submitted after the election because the proposal had not been passed until the parliamentary dissolution. *The Malay Mail*, 11 November 1999, 4.

20 Research and Information Services, *Elections in Malaysia: A Handbook of Facts and Figures on The Elections: 1955–1995* (Kuala Lumpur: The New Straits Times Press, 1999), Chapters 4 and 11. The percentages of UMNO seats in the total BN seats in parliament were as follows: 45 percent in 1974, 53 percent in 1978, 53 percent in 1982, 56 percent in 1986, 56 percent in 1990, 55 percent in 1995, and 49 percent in 1999.

21 *FEER*, 16 September 1999, 22

22 *FEER*, 10 December 1998, 19.

23 *FEER*, 10 December 1998, 19; *FEER*, 1 July 1999. By that time, Keadilan claimed only 150,000 members. PAS was thus a more serious threat to UMNO than Keadilan. In an attempt to curb this increasing power of PAS, Mahathir appointed Tengku Razaleigh Hamzah, former PAS ally and uncle of the Kelantan Sultanah, as Kelantan UMNO liaison committee chair in June 1999, a post that had been held by Mahathir since 1990.

24 *FEER*, 1 July 1999, 18–19.

25 *Utusan Express*, 22 November 1999.

26 John Funston, 'Malaysia's Election: Malay Winds of Change?' in *Trends in Malaysia: Election Assessment*, Trends in Southeast Asia, no. 1 (Singapore: Institute of Southeast Asian Studies, January 2000).

27 *Utusan Express*, 15 July 1999.

28 *Utusan Express*, 8 November 1999. This stance of Nik Aziz, however, was disputed by PAS President Fadzil Noor, who said, 'In reality, there could not possibly be a non-Malay prime minister due to the Malay majority in parliament.' *Utusan Express*, 9 November 1999.

29 For the political trajectory of Semangat 46, see Research and Information Services, *Elections in Malaysia*, 61–3.

30 *Utusan Express*, 21 November 1999, and *The Malay Mail*, 22 November 1999, 7.

31 The data here come from 'Results' in *New Straits Times*, 1 December 1999; *Bernama* at http://bernama.spr.gov.my/. Survey data are unavailable in Malaysia. The district-level data set, on which this study relies, is the best possible published data. It would also be better to see how many Malays defected from UMNO, but UMNO fields candidates only in the name of BN.

32 If the percentage of ethnic Chinese is used, we get a mirror image of the figure, given the small population of Indian and other minor ethnic groups at the district level.

33 *Utusan Express*, 3 September 1999.

34 *Utusan Express*, 6 October 1999.

35 *Utusan Express*, 30 July 1999.

36 The 1996 growth rate was 7.1 percent, but the current account deficit amounted to 23.7 billion dollars. Seoul-based research institutes predicted that the current account deficit would decrease in 1997, and economic growth would continue.

37 After his defeat in the presidential election, Lee joined Kim Dae Jung's party.

38 See note 58 in Chapter 3.

39 When I use aggregate data from the 2000 parliamentary election, regional voters refer, however, to current Kyongsang and Cholla residents.

40 Institute for Korean Election Studies, *Korean Election Study, 1997: the Fifteenth Presidential Election* (in Korean), codebook (Seoul, 1998). The same institute under-took a similar survey with the 1992 presidential election.

41 The election results were as follows: 112 seats for Yi Hoi Chang's party, 96 for Kim Dae Jung's party, and 12 for Kim Jong Pil's party in addition to 7 seats for others, excluding the 46 bonus seats at the national level.

42 The turnouts in parliamentary elections were 75.8 percent in 1988, 71.9 percent in 1992, 63.9 percent in 1996, and 57.2 percent in 2000.

43 Data are from the Korean National Election Commission, http://www.nec.go.kr.

44 Note that the support rate for Kim's governing party dropped in its stronghold after the economic crisis; by contrast, Yi's opposition party (GNP) gained more votes in its own stronghold after the crisis.

45 Political parties' campaign spending data are on the Internet bulletin board of the National Election Commission, http://www.nec.go.kr.

46 Among others, Stephan Haggard, *The Political Economy of the Asian Financial Crisis* (Washington, DC: Institute for International Economics, August 2000); Jongryn Mo and Chung-in Moon, 'Korea after the Crash,' *Journal Democracy* 10 (July 1999): 150–64; and Joon-Ho Hahm, 'Financial System Restructuring in Korea: The Crisis and Its Resolution,' in *East Asia's Financial Systems: Evolution and Crisis*, ed., Seiichi Masuyama, Donnna Vandernbrink, and Chia Shaw Yue (Singapore: ISEAS, 1999).

47 Mo and Moon, 'Korea,' 150–1.

48 Hahm, 'Financial System Restructuring,' 130.

49 Seung No Choi, *Big Businesses in Korea, 1999* (in Korean) (Seoul: Free Enterprise Center, 1999), 43.

50 One of the big five chaebol owners, Kim Woo Jung, did not attend the meeting because he was overseas.

51 Government of Korea, 'Korea: Memorandum on Economic Policies,' an attachment to Korea's letter of intent to the IMF, 27 October 1998.

52 Attachment 4, 'The Five Big Groups' Agreement with the Government and Banks on Corporate Restructuring,' in Sangin Hwang, Yeunjong Wang, and Sengbung Yi, *Korean Economy under the IMF Program* (in Korean), vol. 2 (Seoul: KIIEP, 1999), 298.

53 Daewoo was the second-ranked chaebol before being placed under the workout program in August 1999. On the other hand, the proportion of the top four chaebols' assets to the top 30's total assets further increased in 1999.

7 Conclusions

1 For instance, Richard Robison *et al.*, eds., *Politics and Markets in the Wake of the Asian Crisis* (New York: Routledge, 2000).

2 A recent exception is Stephan Haggard, *The Political Economy of the Asian Financial Crisis* (Washington, DC: Institute for International Economics, 2000).

3 The same phenomenon also characterized Estrada's forced resignation from the presidency in January 2001. His government fell in the face of the people's power, though he was elected with the support of 'the people' in May 1998. He was forced out through extra-institutional mass rallies. Meanwhile, even though Thai elites eschewed populism amidst the economic crisis, they resorted to it later. Once the critical phase of the crisis had passed, the Chuan government's neoliberal policy regime became increasingly unpopular. Eventually, Thaksin Shinawatra, who founded Thai Rak Thai Party in 1998, won an absolute majority in the 2001 parliamentary election through marked populist appeals. Yet, it is worth noting that Thaksin's populism was also characterized by a package of concrete economic policies. This is a key difference that sets Thaksin's populism apart from Estrada's. For details, see Jungug Choi, 'Economic Crisis, Poverty, and the Emergence of Populism in Thailand,' *Journal of International and Area Studies* 12 (June 2005): 49–59.

4 Haggard, *The Asian Financial Crisis*, 45.

Bibliography

Abdul Rashid Moten, and Tunku Mohar Mokhtar. "The 1995 General Elections in Malaysia: A Trend Analysis." *Asian Profile* 25 (February 1997): 33–46.

Abueva, Joe V., Maria Serena I. Diokno, R. B. Rodil, Abrino Aydinan, and Temario C. Rivera. *Ending the Armed Conflicts: Peace Negotiations in the Philippines.* Diliman, Quezon City: University of the Philippines Press, 1992.

Acuna, Carlos H. and William C. Smith. "The Political Economy of Structural Adjustment: The Logic of Support and Opposition to Neoliberal Reform." In *Latin American Political Economy in the Age of Neoliberal Reform: Theoretical and Comparative Perspectives for the 1990s.* Edited by William C. Smith, Carlos H. Acuna, and Eduardo A. Gamarra. Miami, FL: The University of Miami North-South Center, 1994.

Agence France-Presse, various issues.

Almond, Gabriel A. and Sidney Verba. *The Civic Culture: Political Attitudes and Democracy in Five Nations.* Princeton, NJ: Princeton University Press, 1963.

Anderson, Benedict, Takashi Shiraishi, and James T. Siegel, eds. "Current Data on the Indonesian Military Elite: October 1, 1995–December 31, 1997." *Indonesia* 65 (April 1998): 179–94.

Aquino, Belinda A. *Politics of Plunder: The Philippines under Marcos.* Quezon City: Great Books Trading, 1987.

Asia Pulse, 16 March 1998.

Asian Development Bank. Asia Recovery Report 2000. ADB website http://aric.adb.org, March 2000.

Asiaweek, http://www.asiaweek.com, various issues.

Associated Press Newswires, 8 January 1997.

Baker, Richard W. "Indonesia in Crisis." *Asia Pacific Issues: Analysis from the East-West Center* 36 (May 1998).

Baker, Richard W., M. Hadi Soesastro, J. Kristiadi, and Douglas E. Ramage, eds. *Indonesia: The Challenge of Change.* New York: St Martin's Press, 1999.

Bangkok Post, various issues.

Banks, Arthur S., ed. *Political Handbook of the World: 1987.* Binghamton, NY: CSA Publications, 1987.

——. *Political Handbook of the World: 1998.* Binghamton, NY: CSA Publications, 1998.

Bates, Robert H. "Contra Contractarianism: Some Reflections on the New Institutionalism." *Politics and Society* 16 (1988): 387–401.

BBC Summary of World Broadcasts, 24 December 1992.

Bernama, http://bernama.spr.gov.my.

Bourchier, David. "How the New Order Collapsed." *Inside Indonesia* 55, http://www. insideindonesia.org, July–September 1998.

Bowie, Alasdair and Danny Unger. *The Politics of Open Economies*. Cambridge, MA: Cambridge University Press, 1997.

Boyce, James K. *The Political Economy of Growth and Impoverishment in the Marcos Era*. Manila: Ateneo De Manila University Press, 1993.

Broad, Robin. *Unequal Alliance, 1979–1986: The World Bank, the International Monetary Fund, and the Philippines*. Manila: Ateneo de Manila University Press, 1988.

Bullard, Nocola, *et al.* "Taming the Tigers: The IMF and the Asian Crisis." In *Tigers in Trouble: Financial Governance, Liberalization and Crises in East Asia*. Edited by K. S. Jomo. Hong Kong: Hong Kong University Press, 1998.

Burton, Michael and Jai P. Ryu. "South Korea's Elite Settlement and Democratic Consolidation." *Journal of Political and Military Sociology* 25 (Summer 1997): 1–24.

Burton, Michael and John Higley. "Political Crises and Elite Settlements." In *Elites, Crises, and the Origins of Regimes*. Edited by Mattei Dogan and John Higley. Lanham, MD: Rowman & Littlefield Publishers, 1998.

Burton, Michael, Richard Gunther, and John Higley. "Introduction: Elite Transformation and Democratic Regimes." In *Elites and Democratic Consolidation in Latin America and Southern Europe*. Edited by John Higley and Richard Gunther. New York: Cambridge University Press, 1992.

Business Daily (Philippines), 5 January 1998.

Business Times (Malaysia), 16 February 1998.

Business Times (Singapore), 31 January and 21 March 1998.

Business World (Philippines), various issues.

Caldwell, Malcolm, ed. *Ten Years' Military Terror in Indonesia*. Nottingham, England: The Bertrand Russell Peace Foundation for Spokesman Books, 1975.

Carino, Ledivina V. "The Land and the People." In *Government and Politics of the Philippines*. Edited by Raul P. de Guzman and Mila A. Reforma. New York: Oxford University Press, 1988.

Casper, Gretchen. *Fragile Democracies: The Legacies of Authoritarian Rule*. Pittsburgh, PA: University of Pittsburgh Press, 1995.

Celoza, Albert F. *Ferdinand Marcos and the Philippines: The Political Economy of Authoritarianism*. Singapore: Toppan Company, 1997.

Chai-Anan Samudavanija. "Thailand: A Stable Semi-democracy." In *Politics in Developing Countries: Comparing Experiences with Democracy*. Edited by Larry Diamond, Juan J. Linz, and Seymour Martin Lipset. 2nd ed. Boulder, CO: Lynne Rienner Publishers, 1995.

Chan Kwok Bun, ed. *Chinese Business Networks: State, Economy and Culture*. Singapore: Prentice Hall, 2000.

Choi, Jungug. "Philippine Democracies Old and New: Elections, Term Limits and Party System." *Asian Survey* 41 (May/June 2001): 488–501.

———. "Ethnic and Regional Politics after the Asian Economic Crisis: A Comparison of Malaysia and South Korea." *Democratization* 10 (Spring 2003): 121–34.

———. "Capital Flows, Political Cleavages and Economic Policy Choice: Malaysia during the Asian Economic Crisis." *The Southeast Asian Review* 13 (Spring 2003): 383–400.

———. "Strategic Voting and the Effective Number of Presidential Candidates in New Democracies: The Case of South Korea." *Korean Political Science Review* 37 (December 2003): 191–208.

————. "Economic Crisis, Poverty, and the Emergence of Populism in Thailand." *Journal of International and Area Studies* 12 (June 2005): 49–59.

Choi, Jungug, John Higley, Tong-yi Huang, and Tse-min Lin. "Elite Settlement and Democratic Consolidation in Korea and Taiwan. In *Democratization and Globalization in Korea: Assessments and Prospects*. Edited by Chung-In Moon and Jongryn Mo. Seoul: Yonsei University Press, 1999.

Choi, Seung No. *Big Businesses in Korea, 1999* (in Korean). Seoul: Free Enterprise Center, 1999.

Chomsky, Noam. "Indonesia, Master Card in Washington's Hand." *Indonesia* 66 (October 1998): 1–6.

Christian Science Monitor, 9 April 1998.

Cohen, Margot. "Friction Among the Faithful." *Far Eastern Economic Review*, http://www.feer.com, 11 March 1999.

Colomer, Josep M. *Strategic Transitions: Game Theory and Democratization*. Baltimore, MD: The Johns Hopkins University Press, 2000.

Comber, Leon. *13 May 1969: A Historical Survey of Sino-Malay Relations*. Kuala Lumpur: Heinemann Asia, 1983.

Coronel, Sheila S. ed. *Pork and Other Perks: Corruption and Governance in the Philippines*. Manila: Philippine Center for Investigative Journalism, 1998.

Corrales, Javier. "Do Economic Crises Contribute to Economic Reforms?: Argentina and Venezuela in the 1990s." *Political Science Quarterly* 112 (Winter 1997): 617–44.

Corsetti, Giancarlo, Paolo Pesenti, and Nouriel Roubini. "What Caused the Asian Currency and Financial Crisis?" Manuscript, Asia Homepage http://www.stern.nyu.edu/~nroubini/asia/AsiaHomepage.html, March 1998.

Cribb, Robert. "Political Structures and Chinese Business Connections in the Malay World: A Historical Perspective." In *Chinese Business Networks: State, Economy, and Culture*. Edited by Chan Kwok Bun. Singapore: Prentice Hall, 2000.

Crouch, Harold. "Military–Civilian Relations in Indonesia in the Late Soeharto Era." In *The Military in Politics: Southeast Asian Experiences*. Edited by Wolfgan S. Heinz, Werner Pfennig, and Victor T. King. Hull: Center for Southeast Asian Studies, University of Hull, 1990.

Datar, Kiran Kapur. *Malaysia: Quest for a Politics of Consensus*. New Delhi: Vikas Publishing House PVT Ltd, 1983.

Dejillas, Leopoldo J. *Trade Union Behavior in the Philippines 1946–1990*. Manila: Ateneo de Manila University Press, 1994.

Deutsch, Karl W. "Social Mobilization and Political Development." *American Political Science Review* 53 (September 1961): 493–514.

Deutsche Presse-Agentur, 22 September 1999.

Dewan Perwakilan Rakyat (Indonesian House of Representatives) website, http://www.dpr.go.id.

Diamond, Larry, ed. *Political Culture and Democracy in Developing Countries*. Boulder, CO: L. Rienner Publishers, 1993.

Difuntorum, Manuel C. "The Political and Social Implications of the Asian Crisis." *Kasarinlan: A Philippine Quarterly of Third Word Studies* 13, no. 4 (1998): 35–40.

Digital Chosunilbo, http://www.chosun.com (in Korean), 27 April 1998.

Dornbusch, Rudi. "Asian Crisis Themes." Manuscript, Massachusetts Institute of Technology, February 1998.

Dow Jones Asian Equities Report. 3 April 2000.

Dow Jones International News. 11 September 1997 and 23 December 1998.

Downs, Anthony. *An Economic Theory of Democracy.* New York: Harper Collins Publishers, 1957.

Drazen, Allan and Vittorio Grilli. "The Benefit of Crises for Economic Reforms." *The American Economic Review* 83 (June 1993): 598–607.

Economist, January 26 and 2 March 1991.

Economist Pocket World in Figures 1998. New York: John Wiley & Sons, 1997.

EIU Country Report: Indonesia, 3rd quarter 1998 and 3rd and 4th quarters 1999.

Election Commission Malaysia. *Report of the General Election Malaysia 1995.* Kuala Lumpur, 1997.

Enelow, James M. and Melvin J. Hinich, eds. *Advances in the Spatial Theory of Voting.* Cambridge, MA: Cambridge University Press, 1990.

Esguerra, Jude. "The Impact of the Financial Crisis on Labor, Work, and Employment." *Kasarinlan: A Philippine Quarterly of Third Word Studies* 13, no. 4 (1998): 67–78.

Facts on File World News Digest, 18 December 1987.

Far Eastern Economic Review, various issues.

Feith, Herbert. *The Indonesian Elections of 1955.* Ithaca, NY: Department of Far Eastern Studies, Cornell University, 1957.

Financial Times, 15–16 July 1997 and 12–16 January 1998.

Fischer, Stanley. "The Asian Crisis: A View from the IMF." Address at the Midwinter Conference of Bankers' Association for Foreign Trade. 22 January 1998.

Frenkel, Stephen, ed. *Organized Labor in the Asia-Pacific Region.* Ithaca, NY: ILR Press, 1993.

Frieden, Jeffry A. *Debt, Development, and Democracy: Modern Political Economy and Latin America, 1965–1985.* Princeton, NJ: Princeton University Press, 1991.

Funston, N. John. *Malay Politics in Malaysia: A Study of the United Malays National Organization and Party Islam.* Kuala Lumpur: Heinemann Educational Books (Asia) Ltd, 1980.

———. "Malaysia's Election: Malay Winds of Change?" In *Trends in Malaysia: Election Assessment.* Trends in Southeast Asia, no. 1. Singapore: Institute of Southeast Asian Studies, January 2000.

Gagliano, Felix V. "Communal Violence in Malaysia 1969: The Political Aftermath." Papers in International Studies of Center for International Studies, Southeast Asia Series, no.13. Athens, GA: Ohio University, 1970.

Gasiorowski, Mark J. "Economic Crisis and Political Regime Change: An Event History Analysis." *American Political Science Review* 89 (December 1995): 882–97.

Geddes, Barbara. "A Game Theoretical Model of Reform in Latin American Democracies." *American Political Science Review* 85 (June 1991): 371–92.

———. "What Do We Know about Democratization after Twenty Years?" *Annual Review of Political Science* 2 (1999): 115–44.

Girling, John L. *Thailand: Society and Politics.* Ithaca, NY: Cornell University Press, 1981.

Gomez, Edmund Terence. *Chinese Business in Malaysia: Accumulation, Ascendance and Accommodation.* Richmond, UK: Curzon Press, 1999.

Gomez, Edmund Terence and K. S. Jomo. *Malaysia's Political Economy: Politics, Patronage and Profits.* Cambridge, MA: Cambridge University Press, 1997.

Government of Korea. "Korea: Memorandum on Economic Policies." An attachment to Korea's letter of intent to the IMF, 27 October 1998.

Gutierrez, Eric. *The Ties that Bind.* Makati: Philippine Center for Investigative Journalism, 1994.

Haggard, Stephan. *The Political Economy of the Asian Financial Crisis.* Washington, DC: Institute for International Economics, 2000.

Haggard, Stephan and Robert R. Kaufman. *The Political Economy of Democratic Transitions.* Princeton, NJ: Princeton University Press, 1995.

Hahm, Joon-Ho. "Financial System Restructuring in Korea: The Crisis and Its Resolution." In *East Asia's Financial Systems: Evolution and Crisis.* Edited by Seiichi Masuyama, Donnna Vandernbrink, and Chia Shaw Yue. Singapore: ISEAS, 1999.

Hankookilbo (in Korean), 23 July and August 22 1998.

Henderson, Callum. *Asia Falling?: Making Sense of the Asian Currency Crisis and Its Aftermath.* Singapore: McGraw-Hill, 1998.

Herman, Barry and Krishnan Sharma, eds. *International Finance and Developing Countries in a Year of Crisis: 1997 Discussions at the United Nations.* Tokyo: United Nations University, 1998.

Higley, John and Richard Gunther, eds. *Elites and Democratic Consolidation in Latin America and Southern Europe.* New York: Cambridge University Press, 1992.

Higley, John and Michael Burton. "Elite Settlements and the Taming of Politics." *Government and Opposition* 33 (Winter 1998): 98–115.

———. "Elite Transformation in Democratization's Three Waves." Paper delivered to the International Political Science Association World Congress, Quebec, August 2000.

Hill, Hal. "The Economy." In *Indonesia's New Order: The Dynamics of Socioeconomic Transformation.* Edited by Hal Hill. St Leonards, NSW, Australia: Allen & Unwin, 1994.

———. *The Indonesian Economy since 1966: Southeast Asia's Emerging Giant.* New York: Cambridge University Press, 1996.

Hinich, J. Melvin and Michael C. Munger. *Analytical Politics.* Cambridge, MA: Cambridge University Press, 1997.

Horowitz, Donald L. *Ethnic Groups in Conflict.* Berkeley, CA: University of California Press, 1985.

Huntington, Samuel P. *The Third Wave: Democratization in the Late Twentieth Century.* London: University of Oklahoma Press, 1991.

———. "Democracy for the Long Haul." *Journal of Democracy* 7 (April 1996): 3–13.

Hutchcroft, Paul D. "Predatory Oligarchy, Patrimonial State: The Politics of Banking in the Philippines." In *Pattern of Power and Politics in the Philippines: Implications for Development.* Edited by James F. Eder and Robert L. Youngblood. Tempe, AZ: Arizona State University, 1994.

Hwang, Inhak. *The Myths and Facts of the Korean Economic Concentration: The Comparative Analysis of Aggregate Concentration* (in Korean). Seoul: Korean Economic Research Institute, 1997.

Hwang, Sangin, Yeunjong Wang, and Sengbung Yi. *Korean Economy under the IMF Program* (in Korean), vols. 1 and 2. Seoul: KIIEP, 1999.

Institute for Korean Election Studies. *The 14th Korean Presidential Election Study* (in Korean), codebook. Seoul, 1993.

———. *Korean Election Study, 1997: The Fifteenth Presidential Election* (in Korean), codebook. Seoul, 1998.

Inter Press Service, 9 September 1997.

Jakarta Post, http://www.thejakratapost.com, various issues.

Jenkins, David. *Suharto and His Generals: Indonesian Military Politics 1975–1983.* Ithaca, NY: Cornell Modern Indonesia Project, Southeast Asia Program, Cornell University, 1984.

Jomo, K. S., ed. *Tigers in Trouble: Financial Governance, Liberalization and Crises in East Asia.* London: Zed Books, 1998.

Jung, Courtney and Ian Shapiro. "South Africa's Negotiated Transition: Democracy, Opposition, and the New Constitutional Order." *Politics and Society* 23 (September 1995): 269–308.

Kahn, Joel S. ed. *Southeast Asian Identities: Culture and the Politics of Representation in Indonesia, Malaysia, Singapore, and Thailand.* New York: St Martin's Press, 1998.

Kesselman, Mark. "How Should One Study Economic Policy-making?: Four Characters in Search of an Object." *World Politics* 44 (July 1992): 645–72.

Kessler, Richard J. *Rebellion and Repression in the Philippines.* New Haven, CT: Yale University Press, 1989.

Khoo Boo Teik. *Paradoxes of Mahathirism: An Intellectual Biography of Mahathir Mohamad.* Kuala Lumpur: Oxford University Press, 1995.

Kim, Heemin. "Rational Choice Theory and Third World Politics: The 1990 Party Merger in Korea." *Comparative Politics* 30 (October 1997): 83–100.

Kimura, Masataka. *Elections and Politics Philippine Style: A Case in Lipa.* Manila, De La Salle University Press, 1997.

Komisi Pemilihan Umum (General Election Commission). *Pemilu Indonesia Dalam Angka dan Fakta Tahun 1995–1999* (Indonesian Elections with Figures and Facts 1995–1999). Jakarta: KPU, 2000.

Kompas, http://www.kompas.com, various issues.

Krugman, Paul. "Asia: What Went Wrong?" *Fortune*, 2 March 1998.

———. "Bahtulism: Who Poisoned Asia's Currency Markets?" *Slate*, 14 August 1998.

Kunio, Yoshihara. *Philippine Industrialization: Foreign and Domestic Capital.* Quezon City: Ateneo de Manila University Press, 1985.

———. *The Nation and Economic Growth: The Philippines and Thailand.* Kuala Lumpur: Oxford University Press, 1994.

Lande, Carl H. *Post-Marcos Politics: A Geographical and Statistical Analysis of the 1992 Presidential Election.* New York: St Martin's Press, 1996.

Landon, Kenneth Perry. *The Chinese in Thailand.* New York: Russell & Russell, 1941.

"Landscape of Potential for Unrest." Manuscript, Suara 234 (Voice of 234), Trisakti University's Research Center and Research Institute for Democracy and Peace (RIDeP), 6 May 1999.

Leete, Richard. *Malaysia's Demographic Transition: Rapid Development, Culture, and Politics.* Kuala Lumpur: Oxford University Press, 1996.

Leifer, Michael. *Dictionary of the Modern Politics of South-East Asia.* London: Routledge, 1995.

LePoer, Leitch Barbara, ed. *Thailand: A Country Study.* Washington, DC: Federal Research Division, Library of Congress, 1989.

Lijphart, Arend. *Democracies: Patterns of Majoritarian and Consensus Government in Twenty-One Countries.* New Haven, CT: Yale University Press, 1984.

Lim, Linda Y. C., Frank Ching, and Bernardo M. Villegas. *The Asian Economic Crisis: Policy Choices, Social Consequences, and the Philippine Case.* New York: Asia Society, 1999.

Linz, Juan and Alfred Stepan. *Problems of Democratic Transition and Consolidation: Southern Europe, South America, and Post-Communist Europe.* Baltimore, MD: The Johns Hopkins University Press, 1996.

MacIntyre, Andrew. *Business and Government in Industrializing Asia.* St Leonards, Australia: Allen & Unwin, 1994.

————. "Political Institutions and the Economic Crisis in Thailand and Indonesia." In *The Politics of the Asian Economic Crisis*. Edited by T. J. Tempel. Ithaca, NY: Cornell University Press, 1999.

Mackie, Jamie and Andrew MacIntyre. "Politics." In *Indonesia's New Order: The Dynamics of Socioeconomic Transformation*. Edited by Hal Hill. St Leonards, Australia: Allen & Unwin, 1994.

Majelis Permusyawaratan Rakyat (MPR), *MRR Buku Kerja 2000 (MPR Workbook)*. Jakarta: MPR, 2000.

Majelis Permusyawaratan Rakyat website, http://www.mpr.go.id.

Malay Mail, various issues.

Malley, Michael. "The 7th Development Cabinet: Loyal to a Fault?" *Indonesia* 65 (April 1998): 155–78.

Manning, Chris and Peter Van Diermen. *Indonesia in Transition: Social Aspects of Reformasi and Crisis*. Singapore: ISEAS, 2000.

Markoff, John and Silvio R. Duncan Baretta. "Economic Crisis and Regime Change in Brazil: The 1960s and the 1980s." *Comparative Politics* (July 1990): 421–44.

McCargo, Duncan. *Chamlong Srimuang and the New Thai Politics*. London: Hurst & Company, 1997.

McKibbin, Warwick J. "The Crisis in Asia: An Empirical Assessment." Manuscript. Research School of Pacific and Asian Studies, The Australian National University and the Brookings Institution, 25 March 1998.

Mo, Jongryn. "Political Learning and Democratic Consolidation: Korean Industrial Relations, 1987–1992." *Comparative Political Studies* 29 (June 1996): 290–311.

————. "Political Culture and Legislative Gridlock: Politics of Economic Reform in Pre-Crisis Korea." Manuscript, Yonsei University, January 2000.

Mo, Jongryn and Chung-in Moon. "Democracy and the Korean Economic Crisis." Paper presented to the Policy Forum Online of Northeast Asia Peace and Security Network, http://www.nautilus.org, 18 March 1998.

————. "Korea after the Crash." *Journal of Democracy* 10 (July 1999): 150–64.

Moon, Hyungpyo, Hyehoon Lee, and Gyeongjoon Yoo. *Economic Crisis and Its Social Consequences*. Seoul: Korea Development Institute, 1999.

Mueller, Dennis C. *Public Choice II*. Cambridge, MA: Cambridge University Press, 1989.

Nation (Bangkok), 19 November 1996.

National Democratic Front of the Philippines web site, http://www.geocities.com/~cpp-ndf.

National Election Commission (Indonesia). *Collection of Electoral Laws*. Jakarta: NEC, 1999a.

————. DPR-MPR Member Profiles, 1999–2004 (in Indonesian). Jakarta: NEC, 1999.

National Election Commission (Korea), http://www.nec.go.kr.

National Statistical Coordination Board (Philippines), http://www.nscb.gov.ph.

National Statistical Office (Korea). *Regional Statistics Yearbook 1999*. Seoul: NSO, 1999.

————. *Gross Regional Domestic Product 1998*. Seoul: NSO, 2000.

Neher, Clark D. and Ross Marlay. *Democracy and Development in Southeast Asia: The Winds of Change*. Boulder, CO: Westview Press, 1995.

Nelson, Joan M. ed. *Economic Crisis and Policy Choice: The Politics of Adjustment in the Third World*. Princeton, NJ: Princeton University Press, 1990.

New Straits Times, 1 December 1999.

New York Times, 8, 17 January 1998 and 25 September 1998.

O'Donnell, Guillermo. *Modernization and Bureaucratic Authoritarianism: Studies in South American Politics*. Berkeley, CA: University of California, 1973.

————. "The State, Democratization, and Some Conceptual Problems." In *Latin American Political Economy in the Age of Neoliberal Reforms: Theoretical and Comparative Perspectives for the 1990s*. Edited by William C. Smith, Carlos H. Acuna, and Eduardo A. Gamarra. New Brunswick, NJ: Transaction Books, 1994.

Okposin, Samuel Bassey and Cheng Ming Yu. *Economic Crises in Malaysia: Causes, Implications, and Policy Prescriptions*. Selangor Darul Ehsan, Malaysia: Pelanduk Publications, 2000.

Olson, Mancur. "Rapid Growth as a Destabilizing Force." *Journal of Economic History* 23 (December 1963): 529–52.

Ordeshook, Peter C. *Game Theory and Political Theory: An Introduction*. Cambridge, MA: Cambridge University Press, 1986.

Organization for Economic Cooperation and Development. *Financial and External Debt of Developing Countries: 1991 Survey*. Paris: OECD, 1992.

————. *External Debt Statistics: Resource Flows, Debt Stocks, and Debt Service, 1985–1996*. Paris: OECD, 1997.

————. *External Debt Statistics: The Debt of Developing Countries and CEECs/NIS at end-December 1996 and end-December 1995*. 1997 ed. Paris: OECD, 1997.

————. *OECD Economic Surveys: Korea 1998–1999* (in Korean). Paris: OECD, 1999.

Ostrom, Elinor. *Governing the Commons: The Evolution of Institutions for Collective Action*. New York: Cambridge University Press, 1990.

Pacific Exchange Rate Service, http://pacific.commerce.ubc.ca/xr/data.html.

Park, Jungtae. *The Asian Economic Crisis 1997–1998* (in Korean). Seoul: Buki, 1998.

Parti Keadilan Nasional website, http://www.keadilan.org.

Pasuk Phongpaichit, and Chris Baker. *Thailand's Boom and Bust*. Chiang Mai, Thailand: Silkworm Books, 1998.

Pempel, T. J., ed. *The Politics of the Asian Economic Crisis*. Ithaca: Cornell University Press, 1999.

Permana, Sugeng. "Not Your Local Member." *Inside Indonesia*, http://www.insideindonesia.org, January–March 1998.

Philippine Daily Inquirer, 17 June 1992.

Philippine Headline News Online, http://www.newsflash.org, various issues.

Prudhisan Jumbala. "Thailand: Constitutional Reform amidst Economic Crisis." In *Southeast Asian Affairs 1998*. Singapore: Institute of Southeast Asian Studies, 1998.

Przeworski, Adam. *Democracy and the Market: Political and Economic Reforms in Eastern Europe and Latin America*. Cambridge, MA: Cambridge University Press, 1991.

Putnam, Robert D. *Making Democracy Work: Civic Traditions in Modern Italy*. Princeton, NJ: Princeton University Press, 1993.

Putzel, James. *A Captive Land: the Politics of Agrarian Reform in the Philippines*. London: CIIR, 1992.

Rae, Douglas W. and Michael Taylor. *The Analysis of Political Cleavages*. New Haven, CT: Yale University Press, 1970.

Ramos, Fidel V. *Break Not the Peace: The Story of the GRP-MNLF Peace Negotiations 1992–1996*. Quezon City: The Friends of Steady Eddie, 1996.

Reeve, David. *Golkar of Indonesia: An Alternative to the Party System*. Singapore: Oxford University Press, 1985.

Remmer, Karen L. "Debt or Democracy: The Political Impact of the Debt Crisis in Latin America." In *Debt and Transfiguration?: Prospects for Latin America's Economic Revival*, edited by David Felix. Armonk, NY: M. E. Sharpe, Inc., 1990.

————. "Democracy and Economic Crisis: The Latin American Experience." *World Politics* 42 (April 1990): 315–35.

————. "The Political Impact of Economic Crisis in Latin America in the 1980s." *American Political Science Review* 85 (September 1991): 777–800.

Research and Information Services. *Elections in Malaysia: A Handbook of Facts and Figures on The Elections: 1955–1995.* Kuala Lumpur: The New Straits Times Press, 1999.

Reuters World News, 29 April 1998.

Riedinger, Jeffrey M. *Agrarian Reform in the Philippines: Democratic Transitions and Redistributive Reform.* Stanford, CA: Stanford University Press, 1995.

Rigg, Jonathan. *Southeast Asia: A Region in Transition.* London: Unwin Hyman, 1991.

Robison, Richard. *Indonesia: The Rise of Capital.* North Sydney: Allen & Unwin, 1986.

Robison, Richard and David S. G. Goodman, eds. *The New Rich in Asia: Mobile Phones, McDonalds and Middle-class Revolution.* New York: Routledge, 1996.

Robison, Richard, Mark Beeson, Kanishka Jayasuriya, and Hyuk-Rae Kim, eds. *Politics and Markets in the Wake of the Asian Crisis.* New York: Routledge, 2000.

Rodan, Garry, Kevin Hewison, and Richard Robison, eds. *The Political Economy of South-East Asia: An Introduction.* Melbourne: Oxford University Press, 1997.

Romero, Segundo E. "The Philippines in 1997: Weathering Political and Economic Turmoil." *Asian Survey* 38 (February 1998):196–202.

Rustow, Dankwart. "Transitions to Democracy: Toward a Dynamic Model." *Comparative Politics* 2 (April 1970): 337–63.

Said, Salim. "Suharto's Armed Forces: Building a Power Base in New Order Indonesia, 1966–1998." *Asian Survey* 38 (June 1998): 535–52.

Samad, Paridah Abd. *General Wiranto: The Man Emerging from the Midst of Indonesian Reformation A Political Analysis.* Kuala Lumpur, Affluent Master, 1999.

Schwarz, Adam. *A Nation in Waiting: Indonesia's Search for Stability.* St Leonards, Australia: Allen & Unwin, 1999.

Schwarz, Adam and Jonathan Paris, eds. *The Politics of Post-Suharto Indonesia.* New York: Council on Foreign Relations Press, 1999.

See, Teresita Ang. "The Ethnic Chinese as Filipinos." In *Ethnic Chinese as Southeast Asians.* Edited by Leo Suryadinata. New York: St Martin's Press, 1997.

Shin, Doh C. *Mass Politics and Culture in Democratizing Korea.* New York: Cambridge University Press, 1999.

Singh, Hari. "Democratization or Oligarchic Restructuring? The Politics of Reform in Malaysia." *Government and Opposition* 35 (Autumn 2000): 520–46.

Smith, W. Rand. "International Economy and State Strategies: Recent Work in Comparative Political Economy." *Comparative Politics* 25 (April 1993): 351–72.

Social Weather Stations, http://www.sws.org.ph.

Social Weather Stations Post-election Survey, SWR98-II.

South China Morning Post, 1 September 1997.

Straits Times (Singapore), various issues.

Suchit Bunbongkarn. "Thailand's Successful Reforms." *Journal of Democracy* 10 (October 1999): 54–68.

Sung, Daesuk and Jaeyoung Choi. "A Special Interview with Former President Kim Young Sam." *The Monthly Politic and Economic News* (in Korean), August 2000, 34–48.

Sungsidh Piriyarangsan, and Pasuk Phongpaichit. *Corruption and Democracy in Thailand.* Chiang Mai, Thailand: Silkworm Books, 1994.

Suryadinata, Leo. "Ethnic Chinese in Southeast Asia: Overseas Chinese, Chinese Overseas or Southeast Asians?" In *Ethnic Chinese as Southeast Asians*. Edited by Leo Suryadinata. New York: St Martin's Press, 1997.

Syed Hussein Alatas. *Corruption and the Destiny of Asia*. Petaling Jaya, Malaysia: Prentice Hall, 1999.

Tesoro, Jose Manuel. "Islam Has Been a Social and Spiritual Force. Now It Is Helping Reshaping Politics Too." *Asiaweek*, http://www.asiaweek.com, 19 June 1998.

Thai Parliament website, http://www.parliament.go.th

Thailand Development Research Institute. *Social Impacts of the Asian Economic Crisis in Thailand, Indonesia, Malaysia, and the Philippines*. Bangkok: TDRI, 1999.

Thompson, Mark R. *The Anti-Marcos Struggle: Personalistic Rule and Democratic Transition in the Philippines*. New Haven, CT: Yale University Press, 1995.

Thomson, Curtis N. "Electoral Geography of the Sino-Thai in Thailand's National Elections, 1979–1995." *Professional Geographer* 48 (November 1996): 392–404.

Uhlin, Anders. *Indonesia and the "The Wave of Democratization": The Indonesian Pro-democracy Movement in a Changing World*. Richmond, UK: Curzon Press, 1997.

Utusan Express, http://www.utusan.com.my, various issues.

Vasil, Raj. *Governing Indonesia: National Development and Democracy*. Singapore: Butterworth-Heinemann Asia, 1997.

Velasco, Renato S. "Philippine Democracy: Promise and Performance." In *Democratization in Southeast and East Asia*. Edited by Anek Laothamatas. New York: St Martin's Press, 1997.

Wade, Robert and Frank Veneroso. "The Asian Crisis: The High Debt Model vs. The Wall Street-Treasury-IMF Complex." *New Left Review* 228 (March–April 1998): 3–22.

Wall Street Journal, 4 February 1998.

Washington Post, 29 October 1997 and 18 January 1998.

Weingast, Barry R. "The Political Foundations of Democracy and the Rule of Law." *American Political Science Review* 91 (June 1997): 245–63.

Win, May Kyi and Harold E. Smith. *Historical Dictionary of Thailand*. London: The Scarecrow Press, Inc., 1995.

World Bank, *East Asia: The Road to Recovery*. Washington, DC: The World Bank, 1998.

Wright, Martin, ed. *Revolution in the Philippines?: A Keesing's Special Reports*. Chicago: St James Press, 1988.

Wyplosz, Charles. "Globalized Financial Markets and Financial Crisis." Paper prepared for presentation at the conference on "Coping with Financial Crises in Developing and Transition Countries: Regulatory and Supervisory Challenges in a New Era of Global Finance" organized by the Forum on Debt and Development in Amsterdam, 16–17 March 1998.

Xinhua News Agency, 11 June 1997.

Yergin, Daniel and Joseph Stanislaw. *The Commanding Heights: The Battle between Government and the Marketplace that Is Remaking the Modern World*. New York: Simon & Schuster, 1998.

Yonhap Annual (in Korean), vol. 18. Seoul, 1998.

Zimmermann, Ekkart and Thomas Saalfeld. "Economic and Political Reactions to the World Economic Crisis of the 1930s in Six European Countries." *International Studies Quarterly* 32 (September 1988): 305–34.

Index